To Ann

Rewriting the Rebellion

Featured on the front cover –
The armies of Robert Kett and John Dudley preparing for battle.
All illustrations in this book are by the author

ISBN: 9781909796577
first published 2018 by
Poppyland Publishing, Lowestoft NR32 3BB

CONTENTS

1. Foreword by C. J. Sansom
2. Introduction

3. PART ONE. The Background to Rebellion
4. The Protagonists
5. Timetable of Events
6. The Landscape
7. The Camp on Mousehold
8. Kett's Command Points
10. '...of men and weapons...'
11. The Norfolk Hundreds
12. The Campmen

13. PART TWO. Prelude to the Final Battle
14. The Battle of Palace Plain
15. Warwick's Pitchfork
16. Warwick's planned first action
17. The Capture of Warwick's cannons
18. The narrow lanes.
19. The Rebel Incursion, August 25th
20. Blockades
21. The City Defences
23. Destruction of the North Wall Gates
25. The Landsknechtes
26. Sotherton's Mile
27. The Weapons

31. PART THREE. The Battle of Magdalen Hill.
32. The Balance of Forces
33. Magdalen Hill
35. The Rebel Route to Battle
36. The view from Kett's Point
37. On Magdalen Hill, Battle day
38. On the Field of Battle
39. The Battle
41. Kett's Flight to Swannington
42. Other Supposed Battle Sites
    Denmark Farm and Dussing's Deale

43. PART FOUR.
    A full analysis of the Dussing's Deale scenario.
    Doles and Deales, Lumners and Dussing's,
    Ground Surveys.

51. PART FIVE. Robert Kett
    The Man, his Conscience and his Cause
55. The Reformation Oak
56. Chronicles of Deception.
58. Walk where the rebels marched to battle

59. Acknowledgements, references and
    recommended further reading.

Foreword by C. J. Sansom

Having written six novels in my series featuring the Tudor detective Matthew Shardlake, in which I have always tried to portray the social conditions of the lower classes as well as the high politics of the time, and having reached the late 1540s, I decided my seventh novel would deal with a subject often neglected by historians; the massive social rebellions which swept England in the summer of 1549, the largest challenge to the state structure between the Peasants Revolt of 1381 and the Civil Wars of the 1640s. There was rebellion across the south of England from Cornwall to Kent and reaching north into East Anglia and the Midlands. The Pattern of Rebellion was unusual – usually building up 'camps' outside major towns. By far the largest of the 'camps' was that on Mousehold Heath outside Norwich. There are varied accounts of the numbers involved, but 10,000 would seem a realistic figure, to which must be added the poorer people of Norwich who actively supported the rebellion and assisted the rebels' takeover of Norwich itself. Under the leader Robert Kett, the Mousehold camp governed itself peacefully for seven weeks, and took over Norwich. Military training must have been an important part of camp life, for these civilian rebels defeated an army of some 1500 men sent against them in July, and a month later gave a much larger and more professional army of perhaps 10,000 men under John Dudley Earl of Warwick a good run for their money both for control of the city of Norwich and afterwards in open battle on 27th of August.

There has been a revival of interest in the 1549 rebellions in academic circles in recent years, but nobody seriously considered the military aspects before. Now in a major contribution to the study of the rebellion, Leo R. Jary has carefully examined the strategies of both sides. He has shown that the rebels' military preparations for the final battle were serious and professional, and that the battle, which lasted most of the day, was no quick rout – although in the end the superior military technology of the massive government army told. He has also I think decisively answered a question which has vexed historians for decades – the exact location of 'Dussindale'. I am entirely convinced by his carefully considered arguments that the 'northern' site for the battle is the right one. I am deeply indebted to Leo for letting me see a draft of his book, which has much influenced my own writing as well as settling for me the vexed question of where the final battle took place. I strongly commend 'Rewriting the Rebellion' to anyone interested in Norfolk history, Kett's Rebellion or Tudor military technology.

Introduction

At his death Henry VIII left 16th century England badly drained of resources. There was war with Scotland, resentment in many parts of the country about the enforced change from the Catholic to the Anglican Church, and anger about increasing prices. Life for the common people was hard, and riots were commonplace. There was gross injustice and cruel punishments inflicted upon the poor. Traditional farming was progressively abandoned, turning to the more profitable herding of sheep, for which fewer men were needed, so farm-hands found themselves out of work. There was resentment over the arrogance of the ruling class and the powerful landowners who were enclosing common land denying the commoners their grazing rights and the small holdings they had used for generations for sowing and harvesting their own produce. Small wonder then that sown instead were the bitter seeds of rebellion. On the 9th July 1549, Robert Kett of Wymondham, a successful business man and himself a land owner, became the unlikely leader of a small band of rebels. He voiced their grievances, and his small band quickly grew into a strong peasant army of thousands. They marched against Norwich, the second most important city in all of Tudor England; so began the ill fated Kett's Rebellion.

The Norwich citizen Nicholas Sotherton wrote about the failed rebellion, from the first rumblings of peasant discontent up to the last battle. He wrote what I believe to be an officially approved version of events, telling the story as the victors wanted it told, for them to be remembered as noble and heroic, while the vanquished peasants had to be seen as foul and foolish. History is written by the victor, not the vanquished, so rarely does a balanced perspective come down to us, and true to form Sotherton was loyal to the government and the gentry of his day. Other writers, Alexander Neville, Raphael Hollinshed, and Blomefield all refute and belittle the good intentions of Kett, the honourable purpose of the rebel cause, and the solidarity of the rebel army. Those biased reports and much that has been written since, by writers in the following centuries, have become accepted as history by many who feel compelled to take those stories at face value.

It is not the purpose of this book to tell yet again of all the reported actions of Robert Kett and his rebels as they marched to Norwich, or of their experiences in the city or on Mousehold Heath; it has all been told by other Kett enthusiasts. It is instead a challenge to the myths, misdirections and deceits contrived by Nicholas Sotherton and those other biased writers of his time. In this book, much of that has been revealed and dissected.

Ultimately we come to a detailed study of the final conflict. There is much contention and decades of argument about its location, but you will see evidence of where the rebel army really did fight their last great battle against the forces of John Dudley, the Earl of Warwick.

PART ONE

The Background to Rebellion

- Robert Kett and John Dudley, the protagonists
- Timetable of the Rebellion • The Landscape
- Kett's Command points • The Campmen
'...of Men and Weapons...'

This part may be used as a framework for delving into the full story of the rebellion. See the list of recommended books on page 59

 # - The Protagonists -

Leaders of the Rebellion and their army of followers

Robert Kett
Land owner. 'The Tanner of Wymondham.'
Leader of the rebellion.

Miles
Chief Gunner and Artillery expert;
most certainly had military experience.

The Leading Rebels
William Kett, brother of Robert;
Edmund Belys; William Faulk, butcher; Dick Cayme from Bungay; John Flotman from Beccles.

Some of the Rebel Army
Tom Jacker from Lynn, Henry Ruston from N.Elmham, Eli Hull of Blofield, John Harper of Tunstead, Tom Prick from Humbleyard, John Vossell of Holt, Will Tyddle from Greenhoe; Nick Byron, a sailor; John Pipe, Tom Rolfe; Simond Chamberlayne, a smith of Wyveton; James Fortune, a sailor; Tom Clarke, Bill Mowe, Tom Hauling, Valentine Moore, Bob Ede, Reynold Thurston, Bill Heydon, Will Browne, Dick Ward, Edward Bird, Tom Tuddenham. Will Howling, Robert Cott, Rob Larold, John Oxwick, Simond Sendall, Will Peck.

The Guardians of the Law and the law abiding gentry

John Dudley, Earl of Warwick
William Parr, Marquis of Northampton
Commanders of the Loyalist Armies.

Edmund, Lord Sheffield
Northampton's second in command.

Captain Thomas Drury
Warwick's leading Cavalry Officer.

Count Piero Malatesta and Van Valderen
Commanders of the Mercenary Armies.

Knights, The Gentry, and Civic Leaders
Sir Thomas Paston, Lord Gray of Powis, Lord Willoughby, Sir Henry Bedingfield, Sir Henry Parker, Lord Bray, Sir Edmund Knyvet, Sir Edmund Wymondham, Sir Thomas Palmer, Sir Thomas Cornwallis.

Thomas Codd, mayor; Austin Steward, deputy mayor; Sir Edmund Pynchin and Thomas Aldrych, aldermen.

Henry Bacon, Matthew Perker, John Corbet, John Flowerdew, Leonard Sotherton.

Men in Holy Orders
William Rugge, Bishop of Norwich; Tom Coniers, a clergyman; Robert Watson and Dr. Barrett, preachers.

 # Timetable of Events

In Wymondham —

Sunday July 7th.
Celebration of St. Thomas Becket; unruly assemblies; levelling of some local enclosures.

Tuesday July 9th.
Assembly on the Common beside the Norwich road, at 'Kett's Oak'. The rebels march to Norwich.

In Norwich —

Wednesday July 10th.
The camp at Eaton wood; more rebels join the cause.

Thursday July 12th.
Rebels at Mousehold; they make camp on the heath.

Saturday July 13th.
Leonard Sotherton rides to Windsor to advise the King's Council of the threat to Norwich.

Sunday July 14th.
Kett establishes his council at the 'Oak of Reformation'.

Monday July 15th.
The city prepares for a rebel attack.

Sunday July 21st.
Council meeting; rebels offered pardons.

July 22nd-24th.
Rebels attack and capture of the city.

Wednesday July 31st.
The Marquis of Northampton's army enters Norwich. Many rebels retreat to Mousehold.

Thursday August 1st.
Northampton's army defeated on Palace Plain. Rebels return and hold the city for over three weeks.

Wednesday August 21st.
In Cambridge, Warwick with his army assembled, begins a three-day march through Newmarket, Thetford and Wymondham to Norwich.

Saturday August 24th.
Warwick's forces retake the city, but his artillery are captured by the rebels.

Sunday August 25th.
Warwick's forces barely survive more rebel attacks. Warwick's destruction of White Friars' Bridge.

Monday August 26th.
After a forced march, Warwick's reinforcements, the fourteen hundred German 'Landsknecht' mercenaries, arrive in the middle of the afternoon. Late that night, the rebels break-up and fire their camp.

Tuesday August 27th.
Overnight, the rebels march and set their battle lines. Early in the morning, Warwick's cavalry and mercenaries pass out of Coslany Gate; Kett's last battle begins; Rebels are defeated by 4 pm. Robert Kett rides to Swannington. William Kett sets out for Wymondham.

Thursday August 29th.
In St. Peter Mancroft, a thanksgiving service is held. Robert Kett now a prisoner in Austin Steward's house.

Sunday September 8th.
The brothers Kett taken to London and tried for treason.

Saturday December 7th.
Robert Kett hung in chains at Norwich castle. William Kett hung at the Priory in Wymondham.

The Landscape

The topography of Norwich and the surrounding country

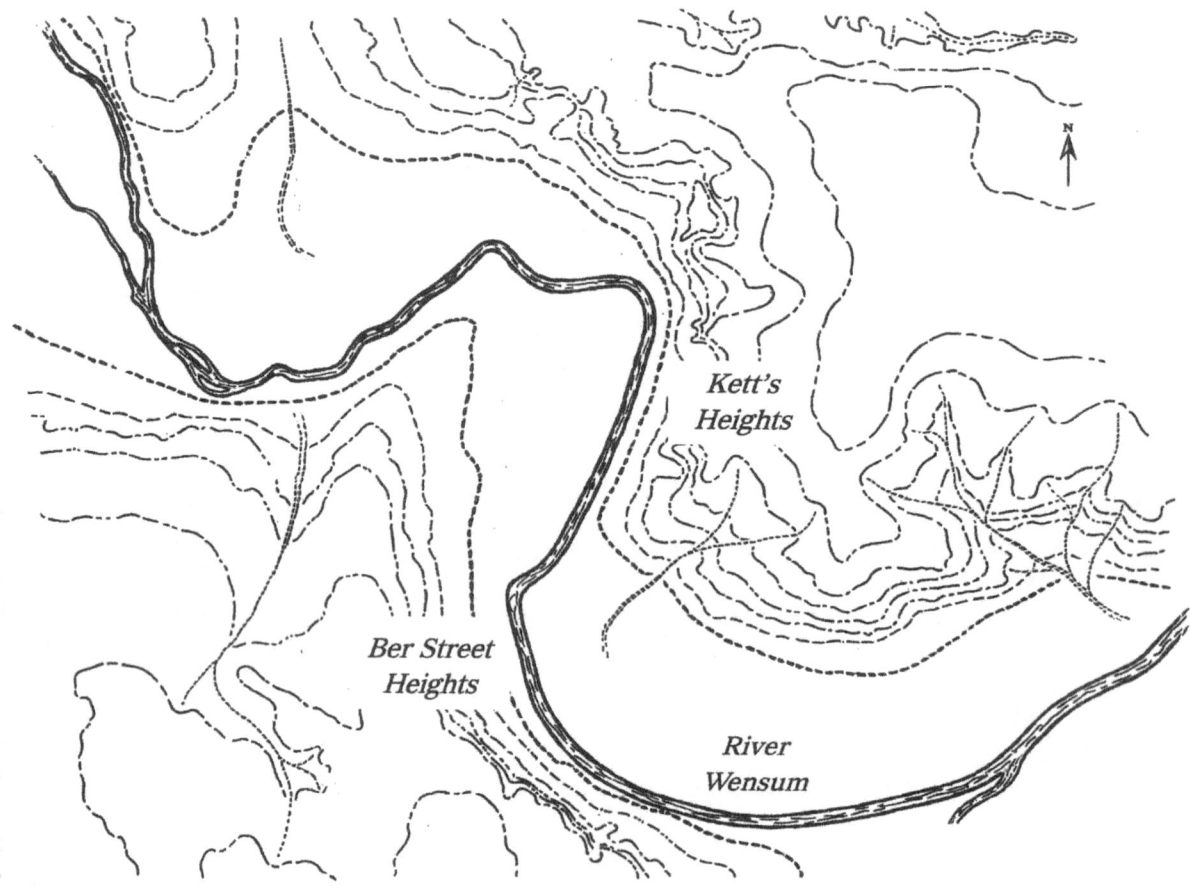

The meandering River Wensum flows through an ancient valley. Powerful erosion has left two steep slopes. On the westward slope is the high ground we know as Ber Street. Atop the eastward slope is Kett's Heights, part of the camping ground of Kett's rebels.

Forlorn and mysterious in a lonely spot on Kett's Heights is one remaining wall of St. Michael's chapel. It had a purpose in the rebellion; it was 'Kett's Castle.' From its westward facing entrance Kett and his leading rebels looked out over the walled city, and planned their brave campaign against oppression. A little to the south of St. Michae'ls, near the top of Gas Hill, is the site of the once grand Mount Surrey, built on the remains of St. Leonard's Priory.

The house overlooked the city and was highly visible. Following the dissolution of the priory, what remained became the property of the Duke of Norfolk, and later his poet-son the Earl of Surrey. It was never finished and Kett's men used the shell as a grim prison for their captured nobles. Today little remains of either the priory or the house.

The Mousehold Camp

Long before Kett established a camp there, Mousehold Heath had become an almost traditional place for rebel assemblies. Centuries earlier, a rebel leader named Lister used the heath for his part in the Peasants' Revolt. Rebels knew that the plateaux-like heights, reaching over 140 feet above sea level, were fairly unassailable, yet well placed for provisions from the surrounding countryside. Its practical advantages being so embedded in folklore, it was understandable that Kett and his rebels would plan to use it as their high ground. They arrived on July 12th. Kett gathered to his cause a number of worthy leaders, and they organised an orderly camp. With so many thousands gathered there, this was no small achievement. They had their own government with representatives from most of *'The Hundreds'*, the major political divisions of the county.

The perimeter of the main military and administrative area of the rebel camp is shown in bold outline. The habitation and domestic areas extended much further to the east, and encompassed Thorpe Wood. Its timber was important to the rebels.

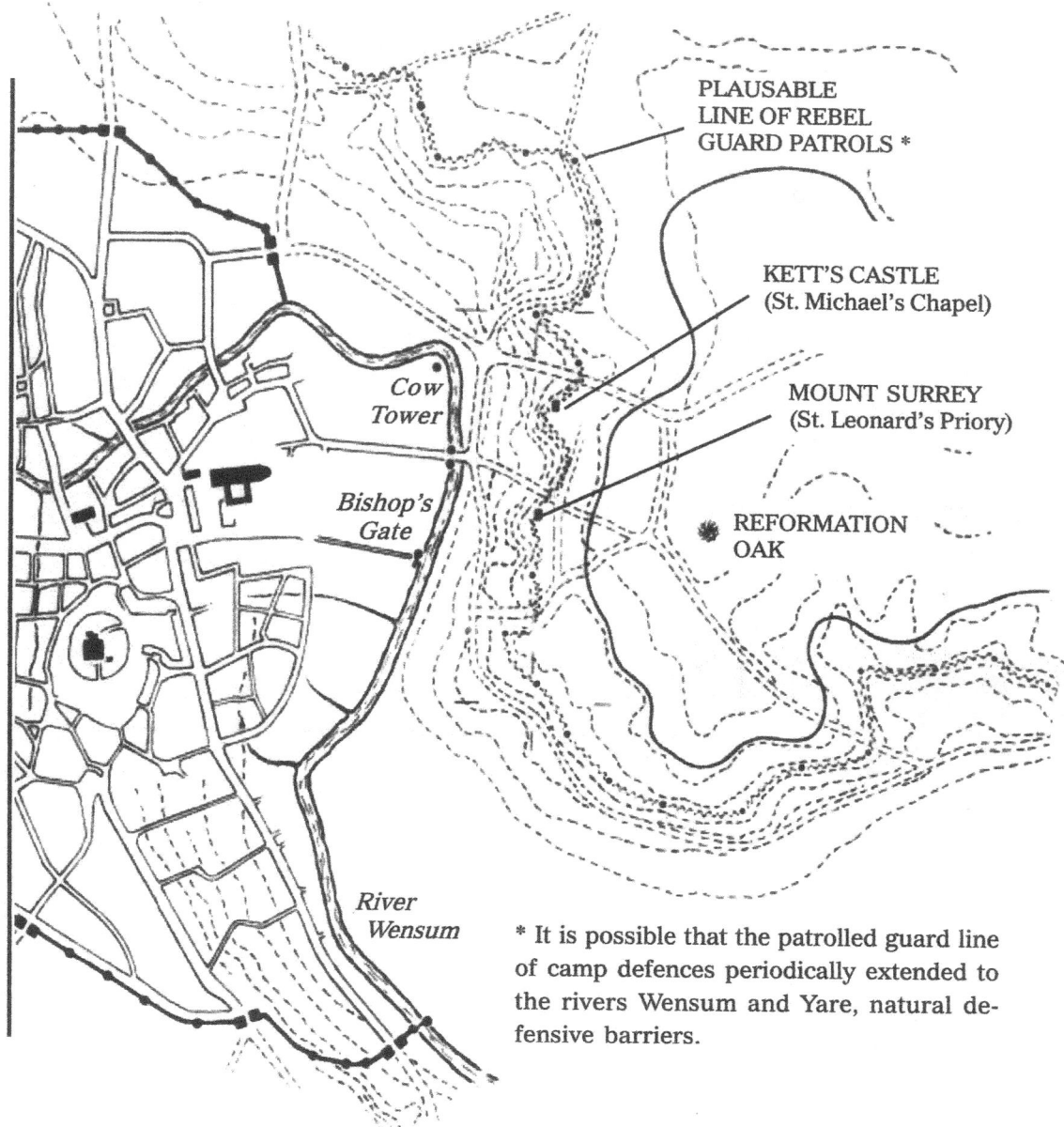

* It is possible that the patrolled guard line of camp defences periodically extended to the rivers Wensum and Yare, natural defensive barriers.

Kett's Command Points

A redrawn section of Dr. William Cuningham's 'Prospect' of 1558.

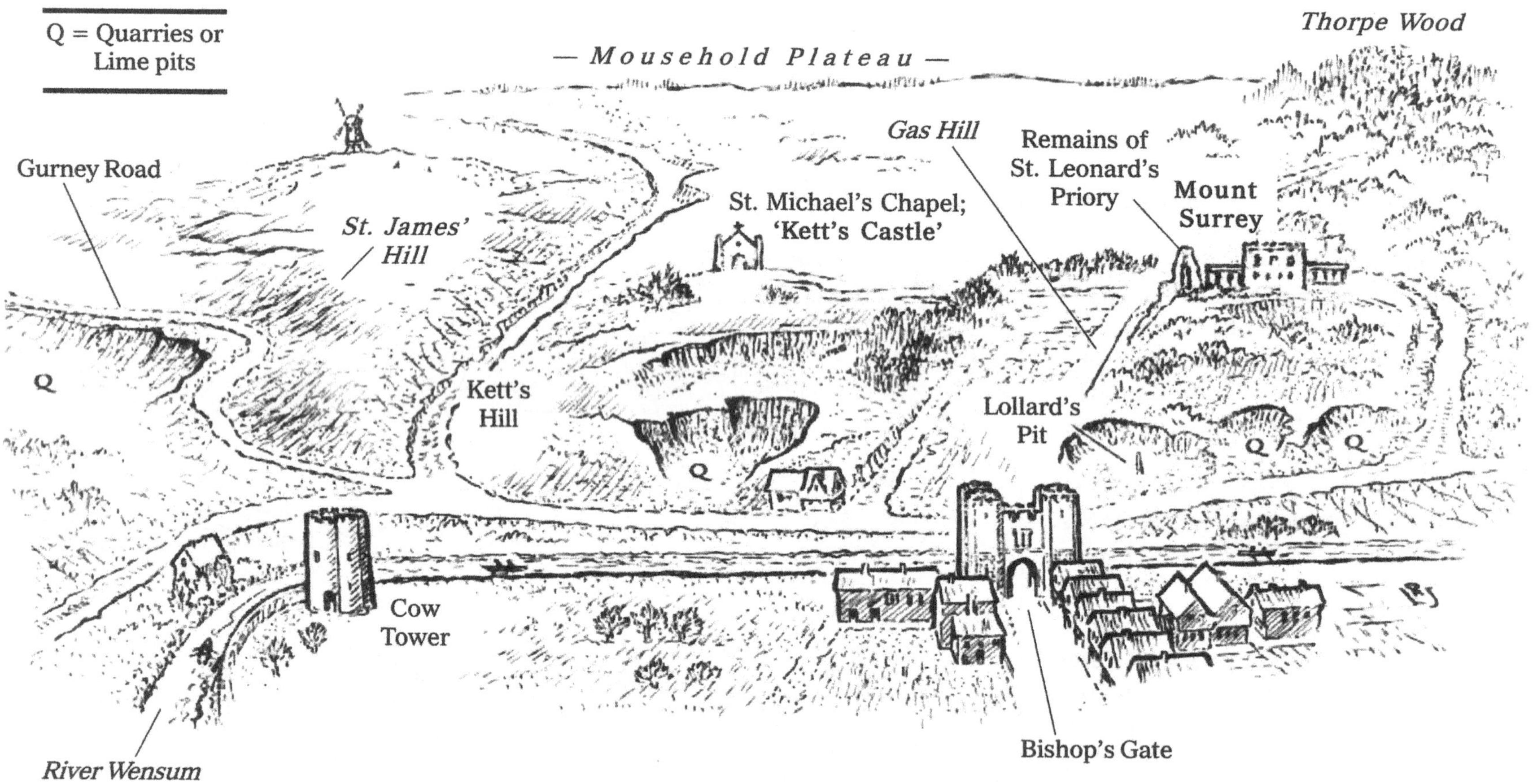

Facing–the one remaining wall of St. Michael's Chapel (Kett's Castle), and the author's impressions of the chapel and Mount Surrey.

The wall is on 'Kett's Height', accessible from Kett's Hill.

Top right; the author's impression of Mount Surrey, based on contemporary and later descriptions. Said to be 'a sumptuous house' ahead of its time, of a style 'more Georgian than Tudor' and 'built at ruinous expense'. The main house was hall-like, with a front porch supported by ionic columns. Temple like pavilions stood at the sides of the house. An ornamental arched gateway was also described, but its position relative to the house is not known. Scant relics of the priory, most notably a small arch in a section of the precinct wall, are on a privately owned site.

Top left; the author's impression of St. Michael's Chapel, with turreted corners.

Left; the one surviving wall of the chapel showing a corner turret. Ruptures in the wall, W, have occurred at weak points, probably where there had been windows. X indicates an added stretch of wall, date and purpose unclear. T is where another turret was located.

 # ... of men and weapons, a great harvest...

It is a common misconception that the rebels were poorly armed, that even in the last battle they had only pitchforks to use against firearms. It is true they had few weapons in the beginning; one sword for every hundred men and some rusting armour. But their weapon stock grew and the number of weapons the rebels were able to collect from throughout the county can be calculated. Of Norfolk's administrative areas, called 'hundreds', twenty two of them had representatives in Kett's camp. Each Hundred consisted of between eighteen to thirty eight parishes, totalling some five hundred altogether, all with towns, villages and hamlets. In those days, such communities retained defensive capabilities, and most stored whatever weapons they had collected in towers, hay lofts and barns. Every parish church officially had arms, powder and muskets.

We may reasonably suppose that most of these parishes gave support to the rebels by providing hundreds of weapons per parish; an eclectic muster amounting to thousands of items, including guns.

Alexander Neville (to underline rebel villainy!) wrote;

'....They brought from diverse parts, all kinds of weapons, a great store of gun powder, guns of all sorts, a great number...'

The rebel weapon stock included old but serviceable swords and armour, old pikes, halberds and bills. Kett's blacksmiths had time to produce in quantity copies of the pikes and bills. At least 50% of the rebels had longbows.

From their experiences in local conflicts, farm hands knew how to turn farm tools into weapons. They fitted scythes and pitchforks with long pike like shafts; chains and threshing tools became flails.

In their raids of the city, they took gun powder, longbows, arrows, pikes, halberds, bills, clubs and staves. In early conflicts they captured artillery, including 11 pieces from William Parr's retreating army. In the last days of the rebellion, they ambushed an army artillery train within hours of its arrival. In that prize were more cannons, and equipment such as quilted jackets, steel sallets and caps. The rebels are estimated to have had 35 cannon of varying calibre.

Kett's gunners, commanded by the much experienced Miles, used their weapons effectively. That required training and skill, involving the making up of correctly weighed powder charges, carefully calculated elevation and range, and the proper preparation of the gun and shot. With too little experience, any attempt to use such weapons was often disastrous. Gunners of a similar age to Kett would have been old enough to fight in the 1513 battle against the Scots at Flodden. Others fought in France with King Henry's renewed campaign there. Alexander Neville wrote in a rare instance of praise –

'Miles, Kett's master gunner, was most skilful in that art...

The conflicts of those embattled years produced many experienced soldiers and sailors who, disenchanted on their return to civilian poverty, were willing to join the rebels.

The Norfolk Hundreds with representatives in Kett's government at the Reformation Oak. Kett allowed two representatives for each Hundred.* There was also rebel support (X) from parishes in non-represented hundreds; those Hundreds are shown stippled and named in italics. The figures indicate the number of parishes in each represented Hundred, many of which delved into their own village lofts to supply the rebels with weapons.

* There was also representation and support from Lowestoft and elsewhere in Suffolk

The Norfolk Hundreds –
their significance during the rebellion

The Campmen

The camp had legal advisors and clergymen to lead prayer meetings, which became as frequent there as in any God-fearing community. Court benches were prepared, huts were built, turf dwellings dug and fences erected. There were soldiers and sailors, bakers and carpenters; so many men, so many skills. To organise and maintain a camp such as theirs, for so many weeks, requires strong leadership and administrative ability. Kett was a good general with a number of worthy leaders. Miles, his chief gunner, * must surely have had military experience, for to use cannons effectively required training and skill; and no doubt there were other capable cannoneers. The numerous conflicts in those battle-hardened years produced many experienced soldiers and sailors who, soon disenchanted by their return to civilian poverty, were all too willing to join the rebels; and such men would see to it that all other capable men kept up the archery practice that the late King Henry VIII had made law.

There were men in charge of provisions, butchers at abattoirs, pens and men herding livestock, which was often somewhat forcefully traded from local farms. There would be no point in bringing to the camp herds of cattle and sheep with no places to pen them, no abattoirs, and no tables for butchering the carcases. Their camp soon covered a vast area, where a good proportion of the heath plateaux was at a high elevation, so there was enough room for all the necessary 'infrastructure' and domestic activities. A rebel named Fulke was a butcher and a carpenter, one of many men with a variety of useful skills.

With a growing number of horses, there was a need for blacksmiths too, who could also turn their hands to fashioning things other than horse shoes; they became weapon makers, turning 'ploughshares into swords' we might say. In the beginning the rebels had few of the established types of weapons. However, a multitude of authentic weapons soon came to the camp, often in the hands of new recruits.

Among the camp followers were women who knew herb lore and remedies, well able to splint broken limbs and bandage open wounds. What little we know of their herb lore, handed down to us through the generations, suggests a profound knowledge that modern science is still rediscovering. This was no primitive settlement; it was a community. When the rebels came to Mousehold on July 12th, they numbered no more than 2600. By ringing church bells and lighting beacons, they summoned thousands more of the poor and homeless, including many the wealthy citizens called 'The scum of the city.' Most of those so called were simply the poor, made so through no failings of their own. The very act of enclosure had brought many of them to destitution. Some turned to violent crime, acted against others in the camp; Such is so often the case in communities where there is desperate need. But Kett's camp had laws as stringently upheld as in any civilised community; hence the setting up of court benches, and the election of a hierarchy of legal councils. Justice was administered and punishments handed down from the benches around Kett's 'Oak of Reformation.'

* It is possible that as a young soldier Miles gained battle experience under the Earl of Surrey at Flodden Field in 1513, then later during Henry VIII's renewed French War 1544 to 1546, and Somerset's Scottish War beginning in 1547. From the 1544 Battle of Boulogne, he would have gained a mastery of urban fighting.

PART TWO

Prelude to the Final Battle

- The end of Northampton's campaign • Warwick's plan of attack
- A planned bombardment • Warwick's ordnance train captured
- A rebel incursion • Blockades • City defences
- Destruction of the North Wall gates • Landsknechtes
- The Sotherton Mile • Weapons

 The Battle of Palace Plain

Kett's men showed tactical skill and extraordinary bravery when facing the first royal army to challenge them. Although they had few experienced officers, there were certainly some skilled leaders in the rebel command structure. Like many of the determined rebels, they knew the city streets well enough to make themselves a problem to the army.

As part of the watch he set over the city, William Parr, the Marquis of Northampton, ordered the lighting of a huge fire in the market square in the hope of lighting the streets enough to deter rebel snipers. He did not have enough soldiers to set a watch on the gates and walls. That duty fell to the citizens, willing or not. Counter to that, Kett set up a trooping garrison in the grounds of the former Benedictine priory, with the same sort of administration as his government on the high ground of Mousehold at the Reformation Oak.

Sotherton plays down the skills and successes of Kett's rebel army; and yet that army made fools of Nottingham's soldiers and mercenaries. The important and decisive rebel success against the loyalist army was 'The Battle of Palace Plain' on August 1st, against William Parr's English soldiers and Count Piero Malatasta's foreign mercenaries. No doubt the mercenaries had fire in their bellies over the wanton killing of an Italian captain, whom a small party of rebels had stripped and hung over the battlements of Mount Surrey. The inevitable battle began at 9:00 in the morning. The young Lord Sheffield, only 27 years old, rode into the full force of the enemy lines, and fell into a ditch when he tried to turn his horse. In the hope of showing his ransom value, he took off his helmet in the hope of being recognised by the rebels, but it was to no avail. He was bludgeoned over the head by a rebel named Fulke, who went on to kill another of William Parr's officials. Some nobles were taken to Mount Surrey as prisoners.

This first attempt by government forces to quell the rebellion has been so well documented by other writers, that there is little need to repeat it here. It is not the purpose of this book. It is enough to say that, although some three hundred rebels died, their fellow rebels won the day. It was the end of Northampton's campaign. The Marquis and his army fled, and Kett's men held the city for more than three weeks. After Northampton's retreat, the movement of their supplies within the county became easier. The rebels were able to scour the county for yet more support, and to set up a scouting system by which important messages were carried to and from the Mousehold camp. That proved to be a wise act; for Warwick, while mustering his army in Cambridge, had pre-armed himself with knowledge of the city provided by Norwich gentry and officials who met him there. By learning from them before the three day march to Norwich, he was able to plan an effective attack. So it was in good time that those rebel scouts watched another army on the march from Cambridge, this time under the command of John Dudley, the Earl of Warwick. By careful observation of Warwick's soldiers on the move, Kett's scouts were able to assess their fighting strength and weapons, most importantly the ordnance in Warwick's artillery train. The scouts then rode fast to Mousehold, and urgently described what they had seen to an assembly of rebel leaders. We may be sure that Kett and Miles, after taking careful heed of the news, made their plans.

Warwick's 'Pitchfork'

Warwick's offers of pardon began on his arrival at St. Stephen's Gate, and continued at the Bishop's Bridge. The rebels declined and Warwick began his attack. It was three pronged like a pitchfork, strangely symbolic of the basic farm tools used by farmhand rebels. The attack by all three 'tines', with closely timed moves into the city, was effective. Their purpose was to drive the rebel troops back, then capture and hold key areas, such as the market square, and the two natural barriers, the high ridge of Ber Street and the River Wensum.

TINE 1. Ordnance was used against the Brazen Gate (1). The rebels had strengthened it but the shots shattered the beams and the metal clad doors. Warwick's second in command, Edward Parr, and his best commander, Captain Drury, led the first force through it to *Alderhalen* (All Saint's Green, G). It is probable that some of this force headed for Ber Street Heights. Others went on to Tombland. Meanwhile Warwick had moved his remaining men to the north, near to the City Wall at Chapel Fields.

TINE 2. Ordnance was used again to blast a gap in the wall (2) for men of the second force to charge through. They swept along *Nether Nueport* (N, St.Giles' Street) and *Ober Nueport* (O, Bethel Street) on their way to the market square.

TINE 3. It is clear that Deputy Mayor Austin Steward had earlier contrived with Warwick for his main force to enter through St. Benedict's Gate, so that the ordnance train could follow that route. The ordnance train was held back long enough for soldiers to march along *High Westwick* (St. Benedict's Street) and *Wymer* (St. Andrew's Street) and secure the city. Then, according to Sotherton, Warwick's third force 'came quietly in through that high street to the market.'

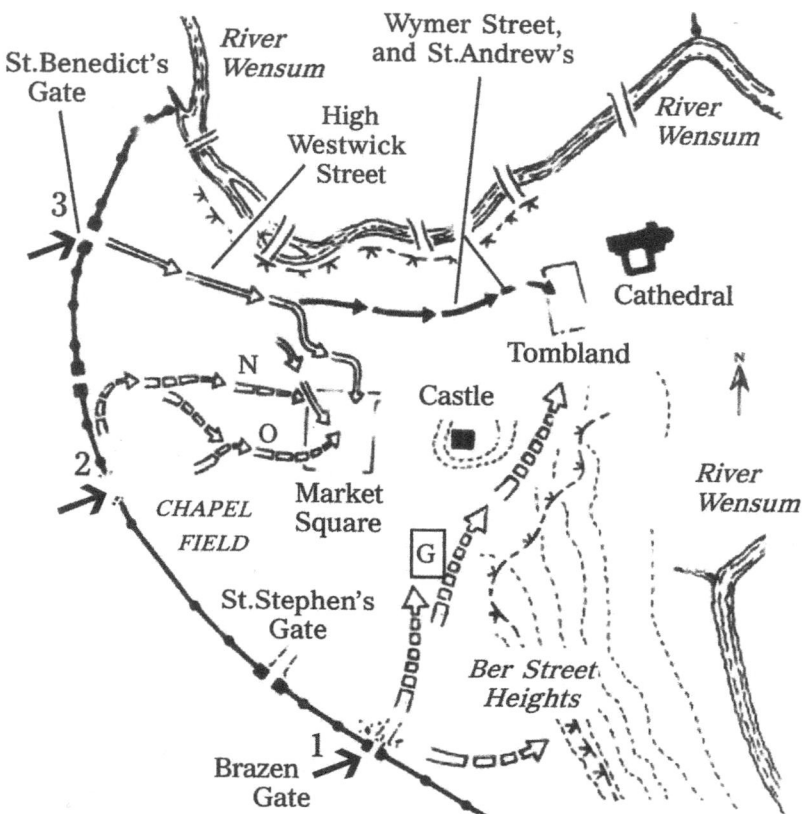

Where Warwick planned to place his ordnance and how he would use it is not explained by Sotherton. It is unlikely to have been the Market Square, that being more directly reached through Chapel Field and the Nueport streets. In the Market Square the guns would have no practical value, offering no clear lines of sight to rebel positions. The only sensible emplacement for the ordnance was suggested by the need to pass through High Westwick, the best route to a carefully chosen site; all clearly understood by Kett's Chief Gunner Miles.

Warwick's planned first action

The intention was to be the immediate bombardment of the rebel camp, by guns placed among the Benedictine priory ruins. The plan was foiled; a subject most carefully avoided by Sotherton.

We may be sure that rebel scouts out in the county watched Warwick's approaching army, took careful note of the weapons in the ordnance train, then rode fast to sound the alarm. I believe I understand what Warwick planned and Miles could clearly see; that there was only one place where Warwick could use such powerful weapons to good effect, and that was from among the ruins of the Benedictine Priory. From there the gunners would have a direct line of sight for a bombardment of the heights of Mousehold. They could be aimed at Kett's Castle, Mount Surrey and the Reformation Oak, then anywhere within the camp. During the afternoon of the day they arrived, they would immediately set the range and elevation of their guns, then fire a devastating barrage into the rebel camp. Kett's high ground would loose all its strategic value.

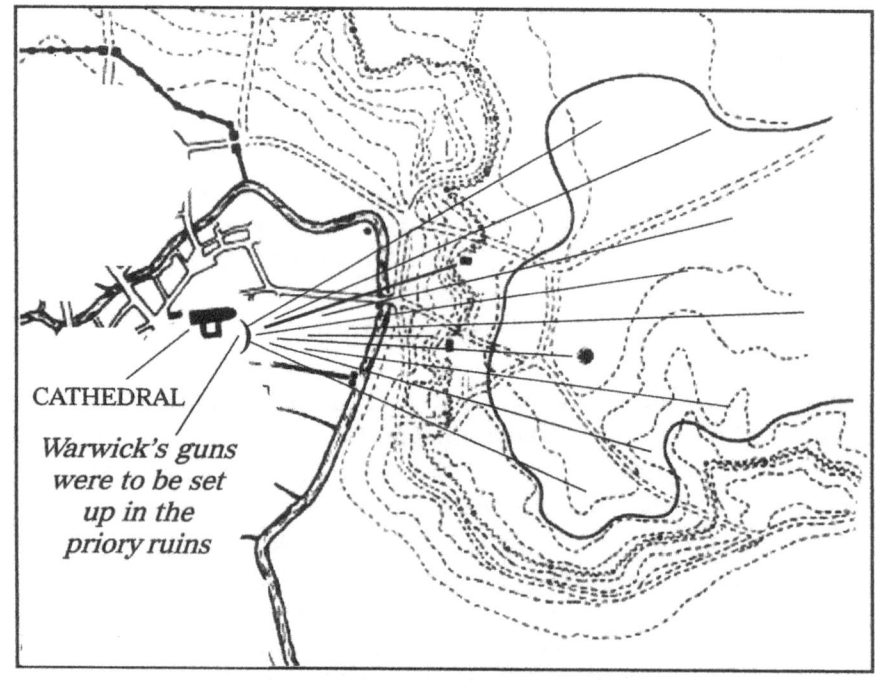

CATHEDRAL

Warwick's guns were to be set up in the priory ruins

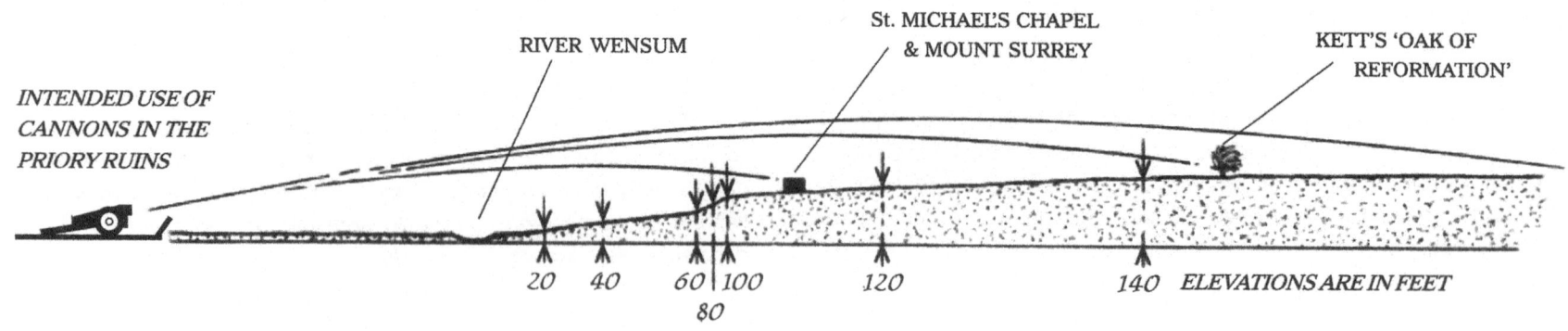

INTENDED USE OF CANNONS IN THE PRIORY RUINS

RIVER WENSUM

St. MICHAEL'S CHAPEL & MOUNT SURREY

KETT'S 'OAK OF REFORMATION'

20 40 60 100 120 140 ELEVATIONS ARE IN FEET
          80

The Capture of Warwick's Cannons

Of course, there was no bombardment. Miles realised the guns would be brought along Westwick and Wymer 'Broad' Streets, the most direct route to Tombland, and from there to the priory grounds. We can be sure there was a hurried meeting to decide what should be done. The rebels had proved themselves to be good street fighters; they could attack the artillery train and capture the guns. Hence the planned ambush in Tombland. They succeeded, even though some of Warwick's men were already there to guard the train. Intense fighting followed, three hundred or more lives were lost, mostly rebels. In Tombland the rebels captured the weapons and supplies. Captain Drury recaptured only a portion of it. We cannot be sure where and how this was achieved. Sotherton; *'...two of the greatest pieces'* were used later by Kett's men. We do not know what guns remained available to Warwick. He had no time to send for replacements.

I suggest that the ordnance train consisted of five field cannons and three supporting supply carts, together hauled by up to thirty horses.

3 It is supposed the rebels took the captured weapons along Holme Street (= Bishopgate, H) and over Bishop's Bridge (B); or possibly along the safer route over Whitefriars' Bridge (W) into the rebel dominated area to Pockthorpe Gate (P).

4 The captured cannons were probably held waiting in the flat areas at the lower end of Kett's Hill, and the heavy horses taken up into the rebel camp for useful service there.

2 The rebels captured the ordnance train in or near Tombland (T).

1 Warwick's ordnance train passed through St Andrew's and along Hungate Street (Now Prince's Street) on the way to Tombland (T).

Deployment area for Warwick's intended bombardment of the rebel camp. The horses were to be coralled on the meadow.

The narrow lanes
between St. Benedict's Street and the Market

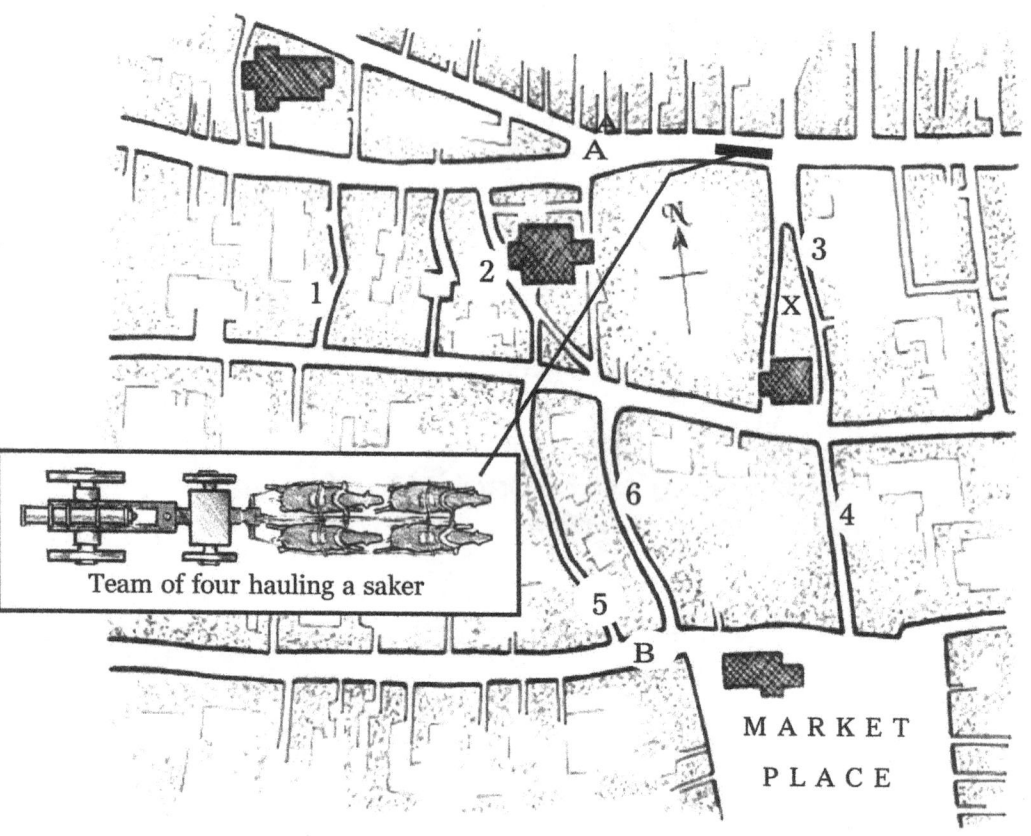

Team of four hauling a saker

MARKET PLACE

The Welsh waggon drivers were correctly on course for Tombland, and the gate into the Benedictine ruins *(The Close)*. It is unlikely that they had lost their way. No doubt the drivers themselves could see it would have been impossible to manoeuvre the teams of horses, wagons and guns off Upper Westwick *(St. Benedict's Street)*, A, and into the narrow side streets *(1 to 6 on the map)*, had they been ordered to drive to the Market Place. (More directly accessible along Nether Nueport, *St. Giles' Street*, B.) As previously explained, they were not instructed to go to the Market Place, as some historians seem to have assumed. The cannons would have been of little use there. If fired from the Market Place, the guns would have been a danger to surrounding houses and inns. The gunners would not have had a direct line of sight to their targets on Mousehold Heights.

We have a clue about the restrictive nature of the lanes. For the visit by Queen Elizabeth I some years after the rebellion, St. John's Maddermarket Lane (3) had to be widened by resetting the churchyard wall further back into the graveyard, X.

1. St. Laurence Lane
2. St. Gregory's Lane
3. St. John's Maddermarket.
4. Dove Lane
5. Upper Goat Lane
6. Lower Goat Lane

The map is based on part of the Hockstetter city plan of 1707. Although it presents the city as it was 158 years after the rebellion, the building lines and street frontages of the lanes had changed very little by then.

The Rebel Incursion, August 25th

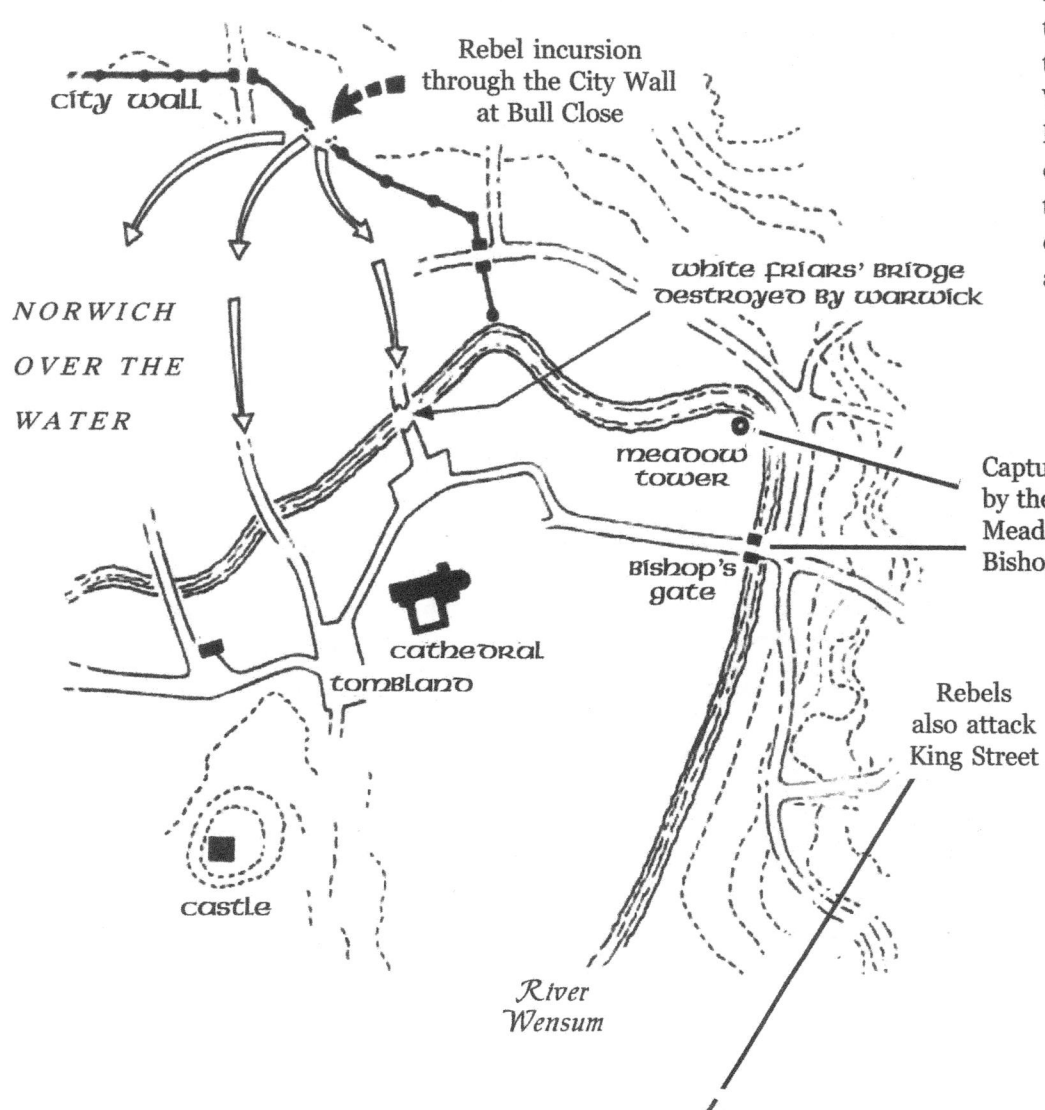

The rebels breached the northern city wall, beside what is now Bull Close Road, and reached the river crossings. The worried Earl ordered the destruction of all the bridges over the Wensum, in an effort to defend the city centre. In the event, the city council allowed the removal of only one, and that somewhat grudgingly. Interestingly, the bridge they destroyed was built of timber; others were stone built, relatively new, and paid for by the citizens. '

The threat to the bridges prompted some aldermen to say they preferred the presence of the rebels to *'...this troublesome army...'* In all probability, Warwick may not have expected to remove all the bridges, a demanding and time consuming task.

The 'troublesome army' resisted the rebels, who withdrew, but Kett was no doubt satisfied that they had worried the Earl and shaken his confidence. Kett's rebels kept hold of the area known as 'Norwich over the water' while Warwick anxiously awaited his mercenary reinforcements.

19

Blockades

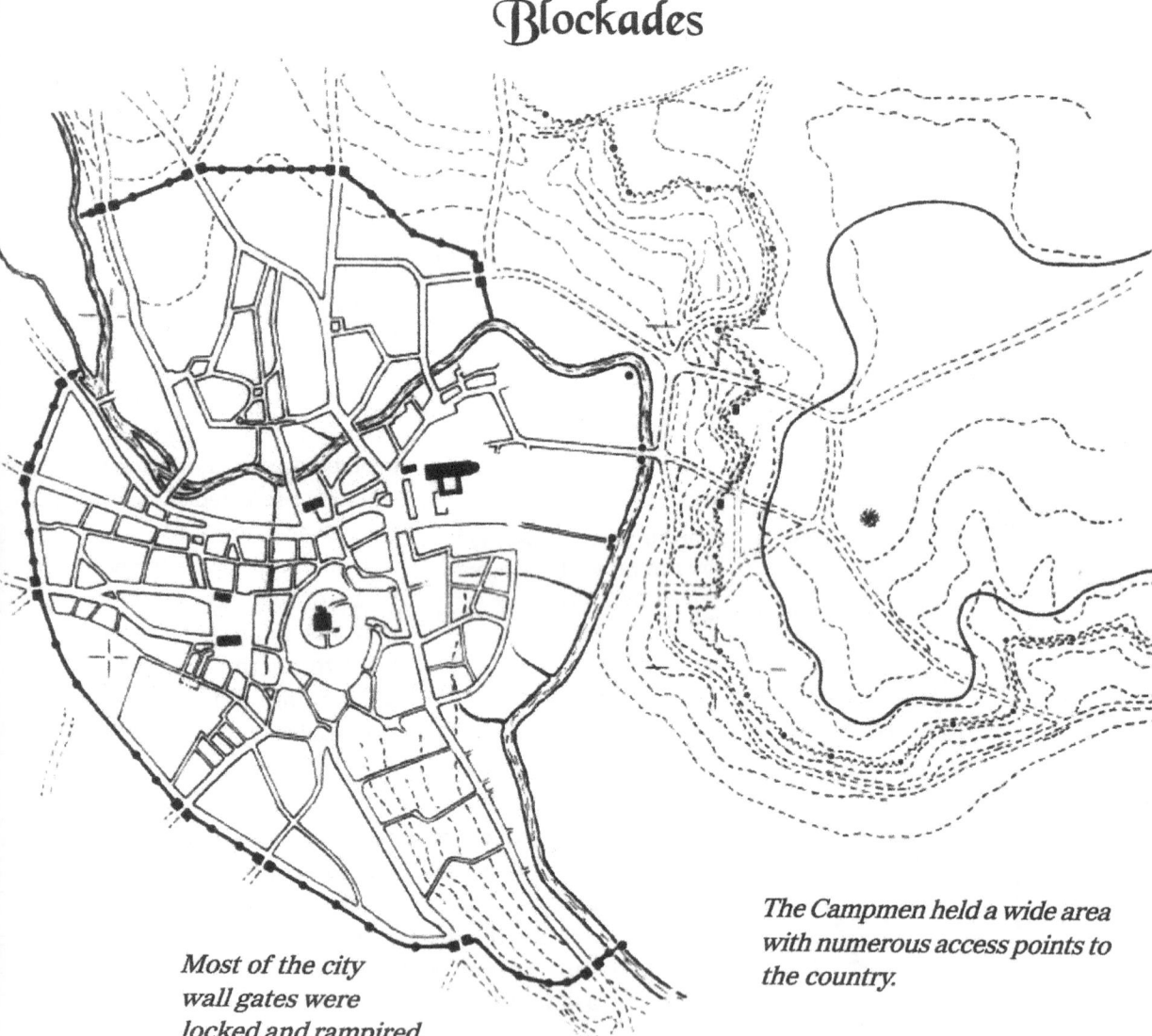

Most of the city wall gates were locked and rampired.

The Campmen held a wide area with numerous access points to the country.

The story that Warwick's men blockaded the rebel camp is one of the chronicler's most misleading statements. The Earl's men held their re-captured part of the city for less than three days before the great battle. While fully securing the city, he could hardly afford to send out enough men to blockade Kett's supply points, which were dispersed along an extensive camp perimeter. The camp extended from five to eight miles further to the east, possibly as far as the River Bure, for the rebels, a necessary supply of water. Warwick could only afford to send out small groups of cavalry to harass the borders of the rebel camp. More realistically, it was the rebels who mounted blockades – at the city gates. It is relatively easy to blockade a city, when most of its gates are locked or earth ramped. Warwick could not allow that to be recorded; so ordered that the blockading story be turned on its head.

It was wise of some rebels to seek access to the market, with a view to enhancing their own sources of supply.

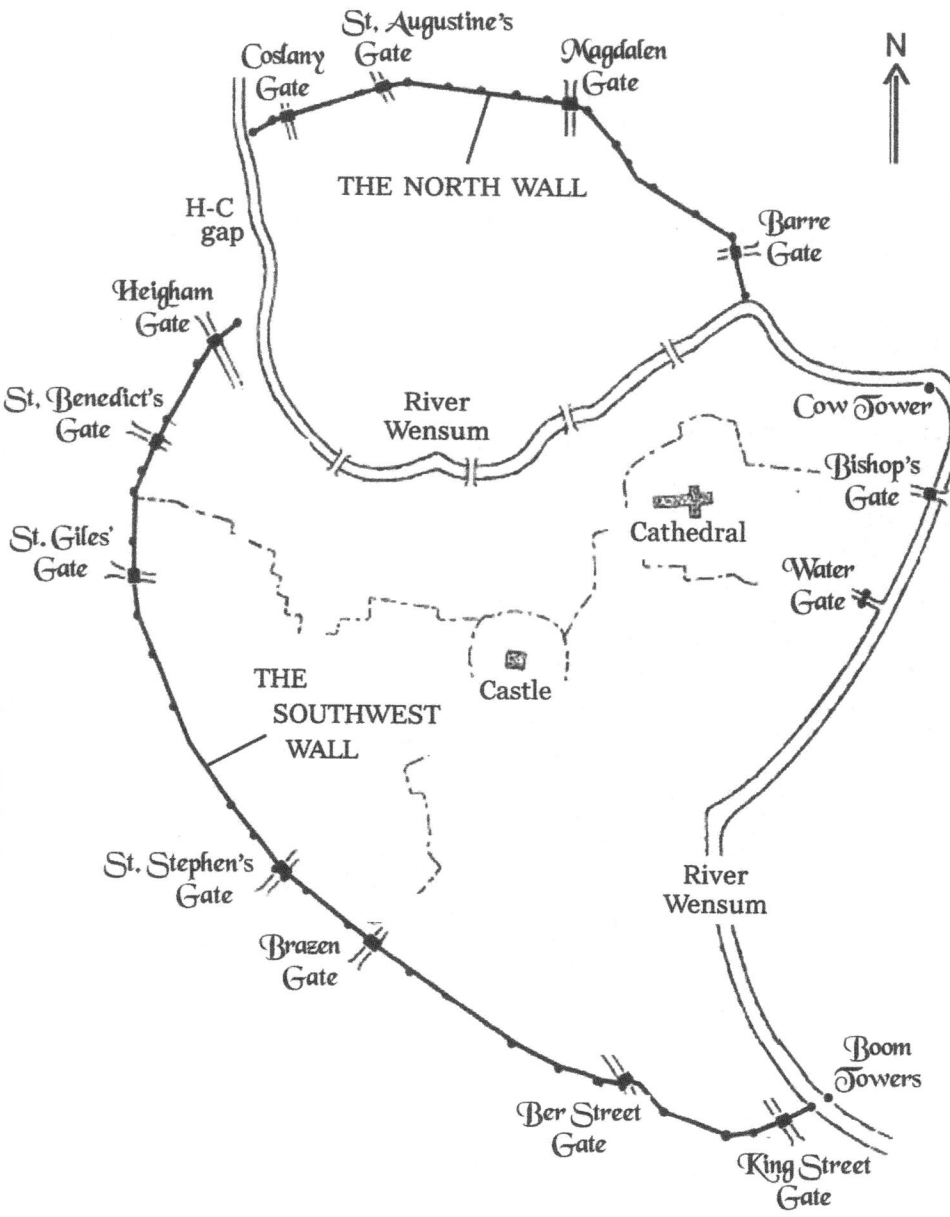

The City Defences

The course of the River Wensum made it necessary to build the City Wall in two long sweeping arcs: a one and a half mile arc to the south and west of the river, and a shorter one of less than a mile to the north of it. The marshy banks of the river marked much of the eastern boundary of the city and were a practical part of the defences, as was the shorter, undefended length between Heigham and Coslany Gates (H-C). Records show that the river was usually navigable for shallow-draught barges and fishing boats, but rarely deep enough for most types of seagoing ships. '

The height of the city walls was generally twenty-four feet, higher than most houses, and high enough, added to the depth of the city ditch, to deter attack with scaling ladders. The Walls had a thickness of about five feet, made up of two leaves: an inner leaf of three to four feet, in which arched recesses *(arcades)* were formed during building, and an outer leaf of about two feet. The outer leaf fully closed the walls, except for arrow slits *(loops)* built into the centre of each arcade. The two leaves are apparent in the wall at the St. Stephen's end of Chapelfield Road. At Barn Road, near St. Benedict's Gate, the wall has fully open arcades; there the wall has almost totally lost its outer leaf. Arcades were up to eight feet high and seven wide.

The City Defences were made more effective by the presence of *'mural'* towers spaced along the city walls. They varied in height from twenty-seven to thirty or more feet.

Preserved examples are the polygonal tower at the junction of Silver and Bull Close Roads, and in the length of wall along Chapelfield near St. Stephen's. There were more than thirty such towers, many placed at bends in the wall where there would otherwise be blind spots. From the arrow slots *(loops)* at their sides, defenders could *'enfilade'* i.e. shoot arrows along the outer face of the wall.

Wardens arranged for the upkeep and repair of walls, towers and gates.

The city gates were built up to a height of thirty-six feet and a width of twenty-one feet. Most were fairly square in plan. Their archways were up to twelve feet high, and no more than eight feet wide; small compared to the wall gates of other cities. Massive oak doors were fitted at the city end of the gate arches.

Men with suitable weapons could launch projectiles or fire shot from the flat tops of the gates. There was much less usable weapon space at the top of the mural towers. The gates had a room above the archway occupied by a gatekeeper. It was the keeper's duty to watch over the gate and the attached lengths of city wall. The room also served as a shelter for guards on wall duty. For them, a small door allowed access to the *'alure'*, the walkway along the top of the wall. The room also accommodated the windlass for winding up the portcullis. For some Norwich gates, there may once have been another windlass for raising and lowering a drawbridge.

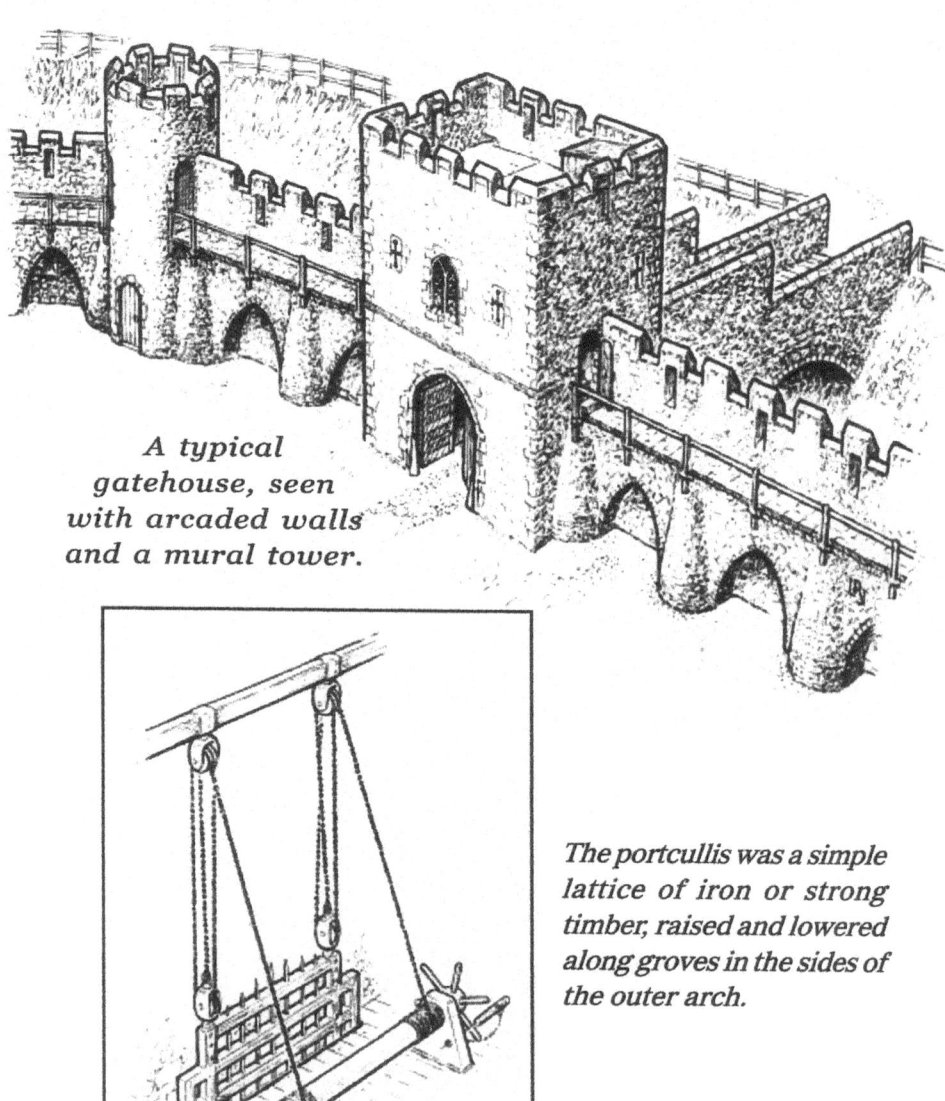

A typical gatehouse, seen with arcaded walls and a mural tower.

The portcullis was a simple lattice of iron or strong timber, raised and lowered along groves in the sides of the outer arch.

Destruction of the North Wall Gates

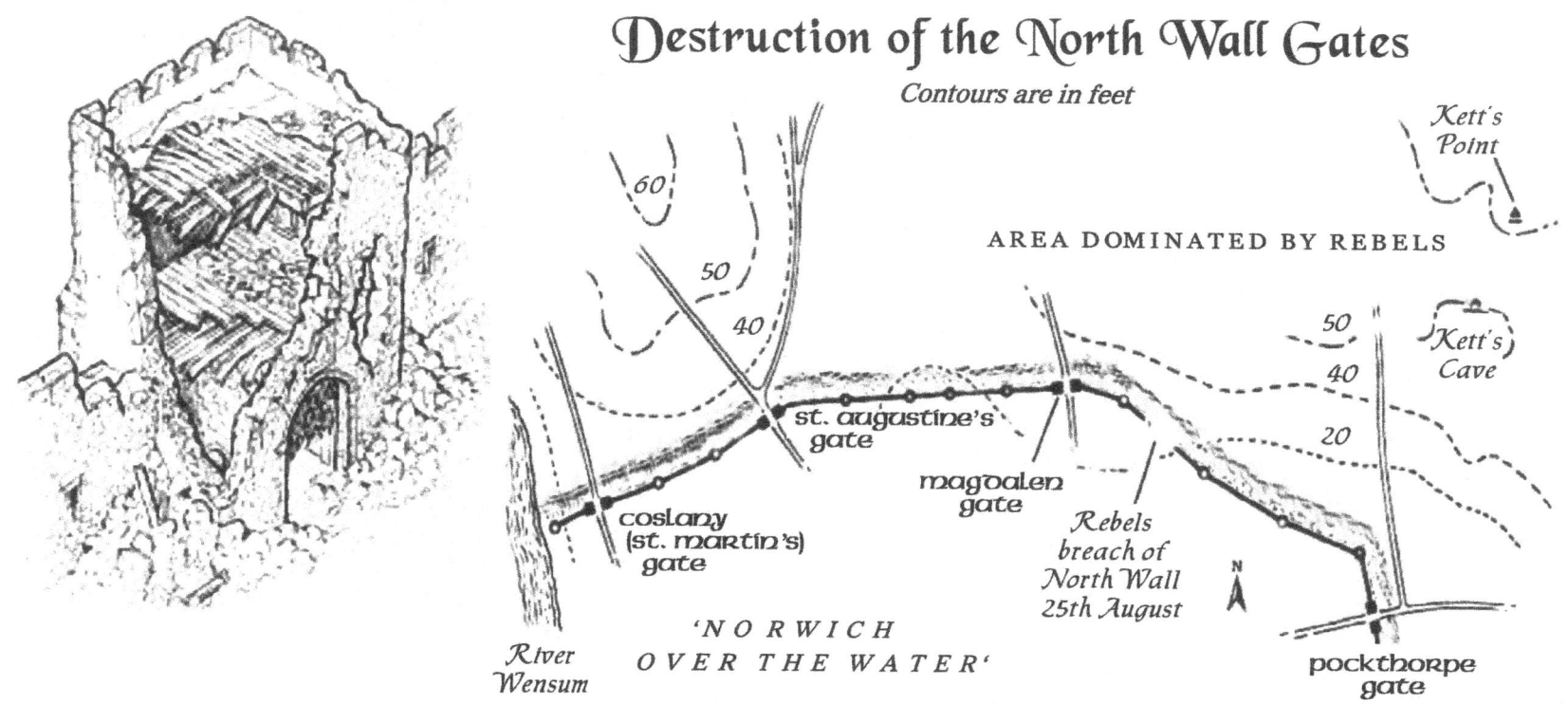

Contours are in feet

Miles would have seen the threat to his men from artillery weapons positioned on the battle tops, and the many 'loops' (arrow ports) in the outer walls of the gate towers overlooking the area the rebels had already decided must be their final battlefield. Clearly the battle-tops and loops had to be rendered unusable. Rebel attacks on the gates are recorded in council documents, although from them we can only guess at the extent of the damage. They tell us more about the Bishop's Gate, how molten lead poured from its roof. Other gates were already weak, previously burned by the rebels.

We have convincing clues about the destruction of the four North Wall gates. John Kirkpatrick's highly informative c.1720s drawings reveal rather more to historians than their architectural details. When comparing his gate drawings of the North Wall with those of the South-West Wall, a distinct difference becomes apparent. Gates of the South-West wall have numerous *'loops'* (arrow ports), while the gates of the North Wall show none. In due course they were rebuilt as economically as possible, without loops; the gates offered little defence against heavy artillery. All were later relegated to tollgate duties.

   Cosn'y Gate   St. Augustine's Gate   Magdalen Gate   Pockthorpe Gate

THE FOUR NORTH WALL GATES WITH REBUILT OUTER FACES
but without replaced arrow slots (loops).

These city gates drawings are all based on the c.1720s works of John Kirkpatrick.

St. Benedict's Gate   — GATES OF THE SOUTH WEST WALL —
                WITH REMAINING LOOPS

                                    Ber Street Gate

  St. Giles' Gate   Brazen Gate

                St. Stephen's Gate

The Landsknechtes

Following the loss of his guns, Warwick depended upon the prowess of these European mercenaries, even though the Landsknechtes were known to have little enthusiasm for fighting untrained civilians.

Urgency demanded a forced march, so it is doubtful that they brought heavy artillery with them; there is no written evidence of them doing so. Even when horse drawn, guns move slowly over rough terrain. These well trained fighters (variously named 'Switzers' and 'Almeins') had to reach Norwich without unnecessary delay; but rebel scouts must have sighted these fourteen hundred men, and gave Kett clear warning of their approach.

The Habsburg Emperor Maximillian I founded the Landsknechtes regiments during his reign of 1493 to 1519. Men were recruited in taverns and local fairs in Holland and Germany; later, more joined from all over Europe. They served in almost every campaign of the 16th century, and became the most feared fighters of the time. Numbers hired depended on the cost; for some campaigns, whole regiments of 4000 men. A regiment, commanded by a colonel *(Feldobrist)*, was made up of ten units. A regimental sergeant major *(Oberster Feldweibel)* planned battle formations.

It seems that England's privy council would pay for no more than three units of a regiment for the campaign against Kett. Each unit was divided into four companies *(Fahnleins)* of 100 men, each under a captain *(Hauptman)*. These were made up of ten platoons *(Rotten)*, each with 10 common soldiers or six of the best double-soldiers *(Doppelsoldners)*, who were paid at twice the rate and were armed with the two-handed six-foot long swords called *Zweihanders*, and halberds up to eight-foot long.

Landsknechtes were allowed to wear feathered hats, wide flat shoes, colourful shirts with ruffled sleeves, tunics decorated with tassels and, as a matter of honour, small trophies of their battles. Only their officers wore full body armour.

Sotherton's Mile

SOTHERTON –

...and carried them (the prisoners) to the said Dussindale with them, which was not past a mile of, and somewhat more, whom to be their defence...

Those lines by Sotherton are more helpful than he may have intended; possibly a truth that simply flowed from his quill in his urge to set down his (or Warwick's) version of events. The words 'Not past a mile' are quite determined in their meaning. The immediately following words, *'and somewhat more'* are confusing but do not necessarily mean that Sotherton went on to contradict himself. With a more careful reading, the true meaning of the whole sentence may be:

"... *carried their prisoners to the said Dussindale, which was not more than a mile away; and further more, to use them there as a defence...*"

By this, he intended it to be understood that there was 'somewhat more suffering' by Kett's gentlemen prisoners as they were taken in chains to the front of Kett's battle lines. Regarding Sotherton himself, we should expect a gentleman of his time to truly know a mile, walking or on horseback. He would certainly not mistake it for three miles, that being the distance along the only practical marching route from Mount Surrey to the so called 'Dussindale.' *(See PART FOUR, 'The other Battle site'.)*

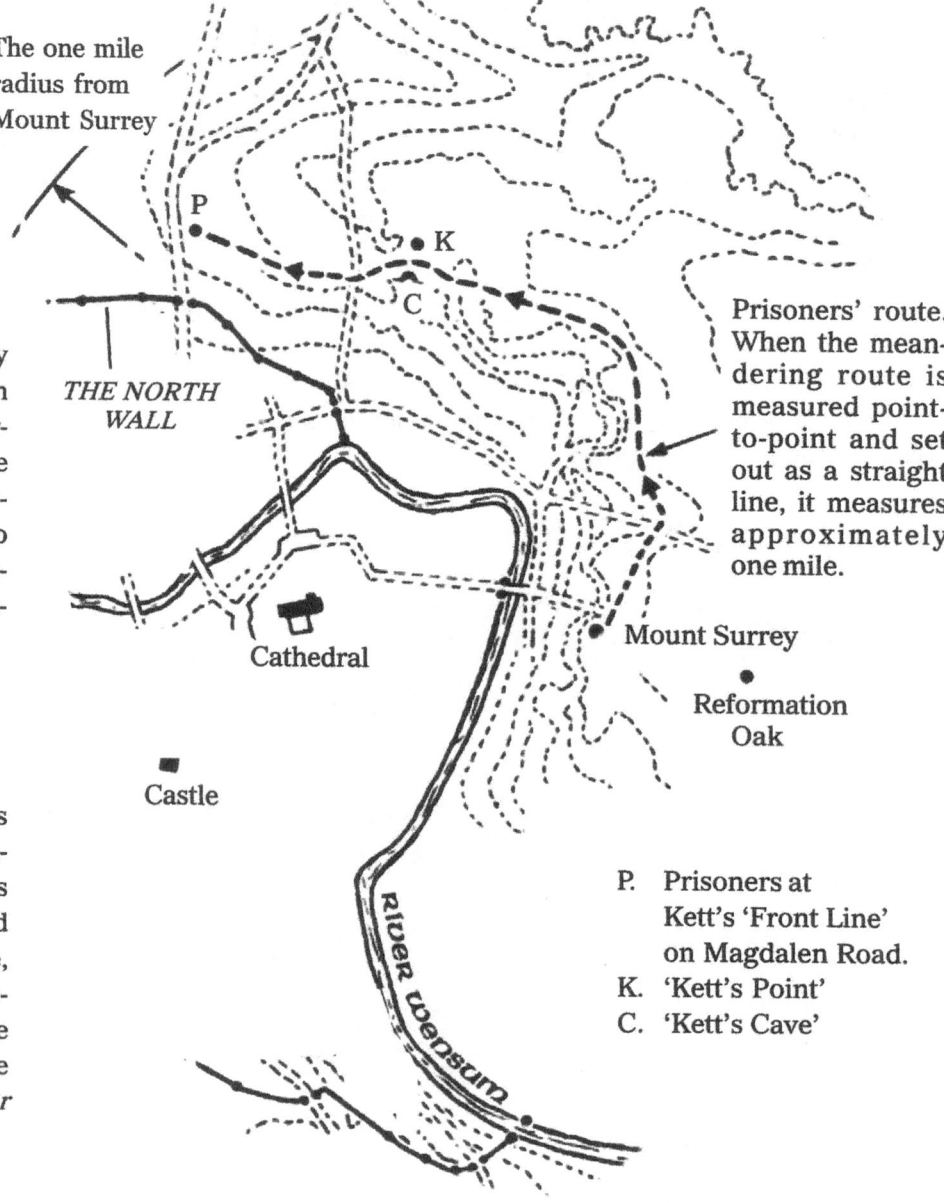

The one mile radius from Mount Surrey

THE NORTH WALL

Cathedral

Castle

Mount Surrey

Reformation Oak

River Wensum

Prisoners' route. When the meandering route is measured point-to-point and set out as a straight line, it measures approximately one mile.

P. Prisoners at Kett's 'Front Line' on Magdalen Road.
K. 'Kett's Point'
C. 'Kett's Cave'

The Weapons

(See the illustrations on the following page.)

Arquebus

Arquebusiers did not aim at distant specific targets; their weapons lacked precision for that. They fired at 'close quarters' into assembled enemy ranks massed at less than eighty feet. Even then, less than fifty percent of the shots fired found targets, and many caused only light wounds, but that high number would have been devastating to the rebels if the volleys were not well countered, which they doubtless were. If aimed at specific targets at close-quarters they were then more accurate than any type of bow. Possible kill range for targets without armour was one hundred and twenty metres; for targets with armour, twenty five metres. Arquebusiers needed to have strong nerves, knowing they were the targets of the enemy while tediously and urgently muzzle-loading their own weapons with powder and shot. To minimize risk, they kept the enemy at bay with a constant rate of fire from their lines staged three or more deep. After the men in the foremost line fired they immediately recharged and reloaded, as the next line of men advanced through the first line and fired, and so on; but if the rate of fire was too rapid, the weapons overheated and exploded, a hazard to other men close by, as were the powder pouches arquebusiers carried.

Crossbows

Some rebels had crossbows, a favourite of North European mercenaries. They were best used as close quarters weapons but were slow to reload. They could not equal the launching rate of a longbow; at most, four bolts per minute. During rewind, the crossbowmen, like the arquebusier, needed strong nerves as they were quite static passive targets when focused on their work.

Longbows

The versatile relatively simple longbows were the rebels' main weapons. These were made from a single yew-wood stave. Ashwood was best for arrows. The maximum practical range for targeting was over two hundred yards, but archers could launch arrows at the rate of ten per minute. A hail of arrows was created when a mass of archers aimed high, creating steeply curved trajectories from which the arrows fell heavily onto the enemy. There was little protective cover. This was the tactic that three times won great victories in the wars against the French, at Crecy, Poitiers and Agincourt, against pikemen and arquebusiers. Obeying the laws of motion first described some sixty years after the rebellion by the German monk-mathematician Johannes Kepler, arrows so launched had a theoretical velocity at the target almost equal to the launching speed of one hundred and forty miles per hour, although air-drag reduced it somewhat. Even so, the hitting power of a two ounce arrow was far greater than the hitting power of a musket ball, and the kill range of a straight shot was up to two hundred and forty yards. There were several types of arrowhead, with self explanatory names regarding their use against types of target, such as broadhead, swallow tail, barbed and forked. A good longbowman could launch nine arrows in the time that a crossbowman could launch only four bolts. Capable men had to keep up the archery practice the late King had made law, so there were many longbows to hand. On Mousehold the rebels had room to practice and learn about elevation and range, and using swords when the battle drew too close for bows to be practical.

An archer's clothes were quite ordinary, except for protective leather patches, most importantly worn along the forearms.

Pole weapons; Bills, Halberds and Pikes

Halberds were six foot long poles armed with well rounded axe-like heads, spear-like points and hooks for dismounting horsemen. They were cheaper and easier to make than most other pole weapons. Bills were similar but without the axe-blades. Pikes were not used for individual combat, nor were they thrown; pikemen, in tight rectangular formations called 'pike blocks' moved forward in a straight line against enemy cavalry and foot soldiers. They were very effective, but a pike block could only change direction with the pikes raised vertically, and its formation was easily broken from the flanks. They were vulnerable to arrow storms. Ash pikes could be more than twelve feet long, so when lowered for battle advance, it was critical where they were held along the length of their shafts, and how the pikemen stepped and thrust. Pike blocks were becoming outmoded by the 1500s.

Most of these weapons were 'harvested' by the rebels earlier in their campaign; many would have been used as patterns by Kett's blacksmiths. There were many implements adapted by the rebellion-eager farm labourers; pitchforks, scythes, picks, chains and threshing tools. Some of Warwick's soldiers, however well trained, may have found it difficult to do combat against such bizarre weapons.

'Shield Wall' Stakes

Rows of stakes well dug in and carefully angled made formidable barriers and, with deep trenches behind them, were an imitation of the 'shield walls' of earlier centuries.

Weapons, from top to bottom; longbow, pole weapons, sword, arquebus and crossbow.

Cannons *The title 'cannon' was not used until the late 1600s. Although historically too early, it is sometimes used in this book to distinguish them from hand held firearms.*

Cannons had earlier been mounted on massive wooden trucks with small iron wheels, satisfactory for use on castle battlements and the gun decks of warships, but so mounted they were not easily transported to battle fields. When horse or oxen drawn wide wheel carriages became available, big guns could be rapidly deployed. The big wheels of sakers and robins, for example, were excellent for transport across country. At about this time there was standardisation of methods for mounting and elevating the guns and the tools and instruments used by gunners; the copper loading scoop, ramrod, barrel cleaning wool-wad on a pole, cooling cloths and dipping-bucket. Iron cannon balls had standardised calibres, and instruments, such as a gunner's scale, gunner's quadrant, height scale and sighting rule were made to prescribed patterns. Formalised too were the gunners' crew stations, arrived at through battlefield experience. No doubt Kett's master gunner, Miles, made sure his gunners positioned themselves correctly and properly prepared their guns. The ground had to be levelled for 'settling' the gun; the long after-portion of the gun carriage, the 'trail', had to be securely anchored to limit recoil. Excessive recoil and gun-bounce reduce the power of a shot, waste energy and was dangerous for the gun crew.

Some historians find it hard to accept that Warwick could be victorious with so few cannons, and choose to believe he had several; but they could only believe that if persuaded that Captain Drury had recovered most of those stolen. Sotherton rather tentatively states that Captain Drury recovered some of Warwick's ordnance and supplies.

He did not elaborate, even though he must have known what little was recovered. Later writers felt free to honour Captain Drury by telling us that most were recaptured. In Blomefield's history, we are told Drury recovered all of the snatched artillery. But Blomefield wrote some two hundred years after the event, when the truth in handed-down memories had somewhat dulled.

The few cannon Warwick had, he probably placed in traditional positions at the flanks of his lines. That was not a good place for gun crews, for so placed they were clear targets for enemy marksmen. I believe Kett's chief gunner Miles understood that and placed most of his guns well to the rear of his rebel lines.

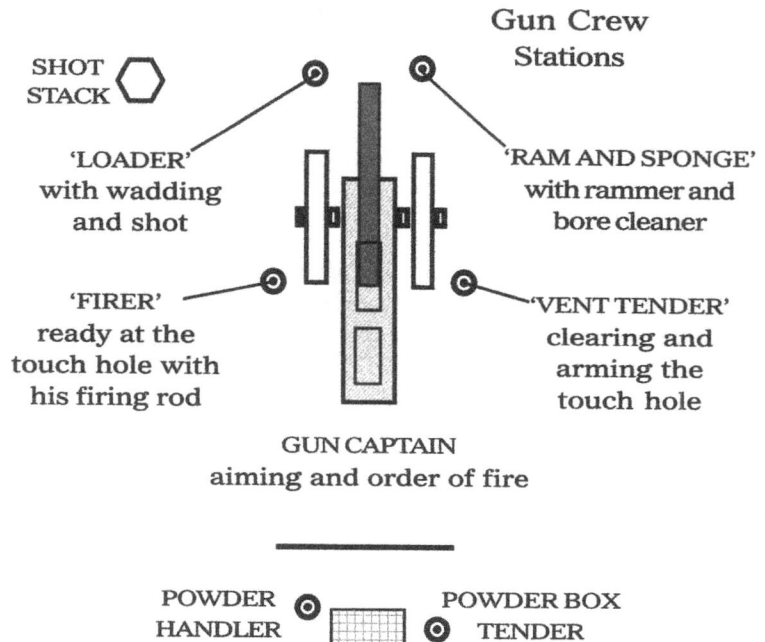

Gun Crew Stations

SHOT STACK

'LOADER' with wadding and shot

'RAM AND SPONGE' with rammer and bore cleaner

'FIRER' ready at the touch hole with his firing rod

'VENT TENDER' clearing and arming the touch hole

GUN CAPTAIN aiming and order of fire

POWDER HANDLER   POWDER BOX TENDER

A truck mounted gun for fortress and warship gun deck installations. There is an example in the grounds of the Great Hospital in Bishop's Gate. Truck mounts were not practical for battlefield cannons.

Captured battlefield cannons set up by the rebels on the Crome Road 'Gun Flat.'

Field Guns favoured at the time of the Rebellion

Records reveal sixteen types of gun. Listed in the chart are average figures for those most probably captured and used by the rebels.

* Some carriage wheels were fitted as available, but had to suit the 'all-up' weight of gun and carriage. Diameters are approximate.

Type of gun by common name	Weight of shot (lbs)	Shot size (ins)	Charge weight (lbs)	Barrel weight (lbs)	Barrel length (feet)	Range at max. charge	Transport	* Carriage wheel diameters
saker	5.25	4	5.5	1500	9.5	3750 ft	5 horses	4 to 5 ft
saker/drake	Musket, grape, or 3.25 ins. shot		5	1200	6	3500 ft	4 horses	4 to 5 ft
falcon	2.5	3	3	700	7 – 8	3000 ft	3 horses	4 ft
falconet	1.75	2	2	500	6	2300 ft	2 horses	4 ft
robinet	0.75	1.25	1	120	3	1600 ft	1 horse or 3 men	3.5 ft

PART THREE

The Battle of Magdalen Hill

- Magdalen Hill • The Rebel's Route to battle • Kett's point
- Magdalen Hill on Battle day • The Balance of forces
- The Field of Battle • The Battle • Kett's Flight

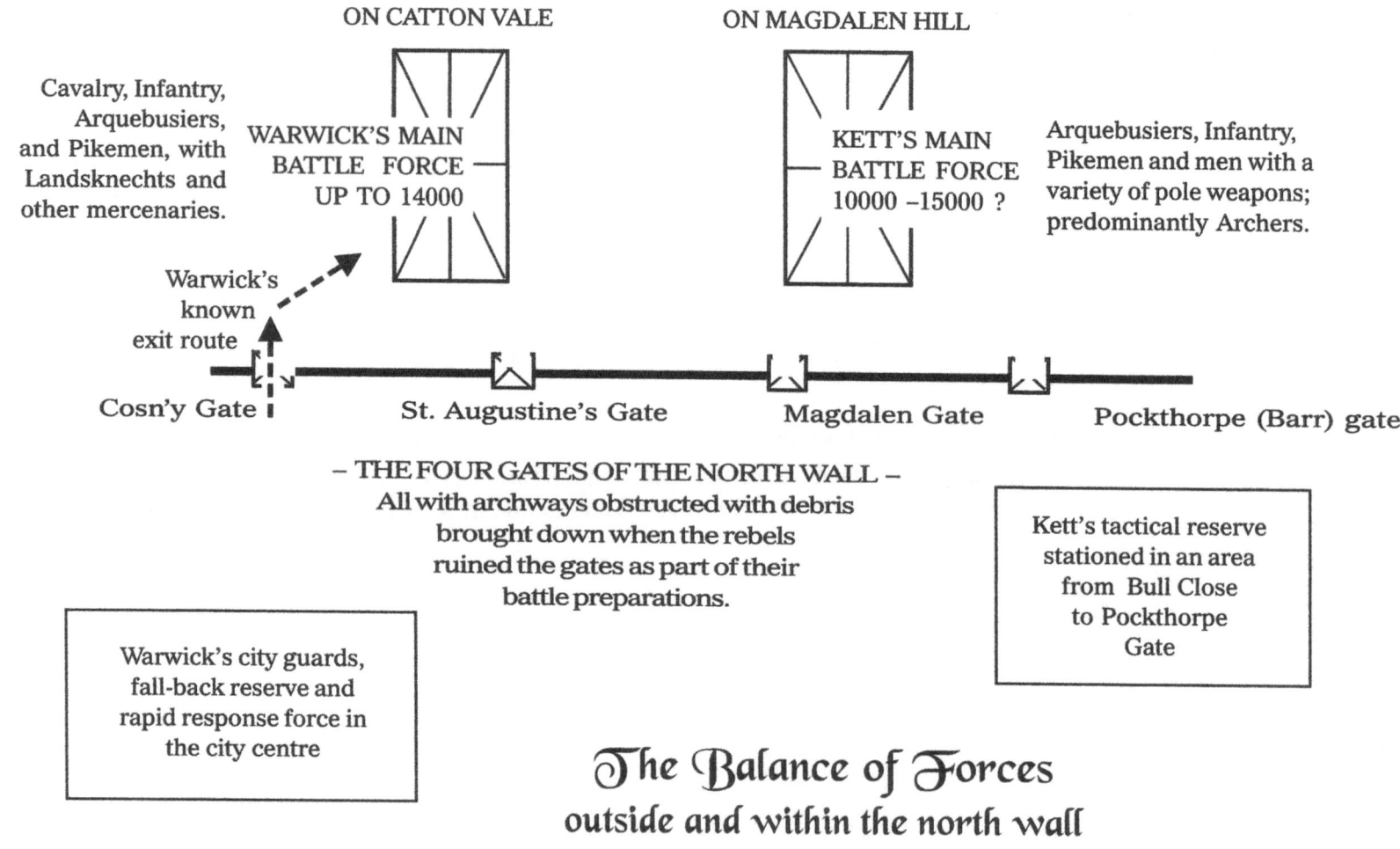

Magdalen Hill

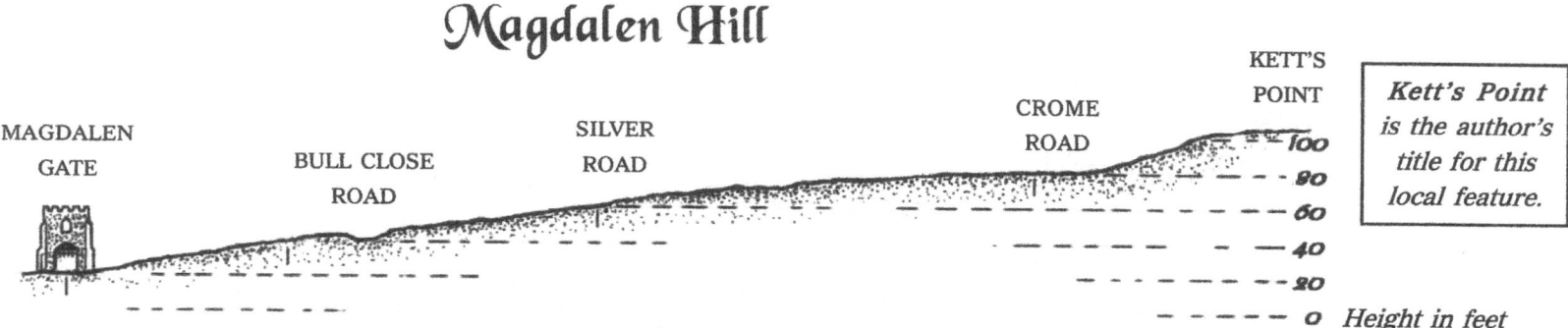

Kett's Point is the author's title for this local feature.

Historians have long argued over the true location of Kett's last stand against the forces of John Dudley Earl of Warwick. Over the years a number of sites have been suggested, including Sprowston Road*, the ground outside Pockthorpe Gate and in more recent years the so-called Dussindale.* Some years before writing about the rebellion, I decided to clear my mind of all the suggested locations and with some understanding I gained over the years from my work with the Ministry of Defence, I replayed the battle as I know many commanders would play it. I looked for a location in strategic and tactical terms, with regard to such factors as terrain topography, command observation and communication points, possible obstructions to troop movements, approach and withdrawal routes and the placing of reserves. In time, what I now believe to be the real battle ground became clear. I walked and measured marching distances and thoroughly examined the topography. And that is how I came at last to Magdalen Hill. I have since learned that some historians in Victorian times considered almost the same site.

Magdalen Hill is a spur of ground over one hundred feet above sea level at its highest point, projecting westward from Mousehold. Kett and his men knew the area well; they passed close to it and over it during their march to Mousehold at the very beginning of their campaign, and they used it when they had command of the city. It overlooks Catton Vale and lays to the northeast of the North Wall. The ground around Catton Vale and Magdalen Gate is twenty feet above sea level and on that the wall and gate towers stood from twenty to thirty feet high. Standing over it all, the hill slope had a commanding position for any army holding it; an ideal location, offering the best tactical advantages to their rebel army, yet easily reached from the rebel camp on Mousehold by marching first over flat ground with no significant humps and hollows, then finally onto Magdalen's westward slope. Its most forward line is about one mile from the command centre of Kett's camp, as Sotherton's 16th century chronicle tells us. There was no better location for the rebels, but it must have seemed daunting to Warwick's soldiers as they marched out onto Catton Vale to face them.

* For an alternative site near to Magdalen Hill, refer to page 42.
  For a full assessment of the much talked about Dussindale, refer to PART FOUR, page 43 onward.

The movement of so many men and so much material from their camp to Magdalen Hill needed careful planning, the work of long hours and many days. You may be sure that when finally agreed upon, the leaders of the rebel force kept its location very much to themselves. The men would have been told only enough to make sensible preparations – and allow or instruct them to spread rumours. The loose tongues of otherwise loyal men have always been a problem, but they can be put to good use; there was the need to allow confusing stories about time, place and tactics to reach the enemy. Even as the rebels 'dug in' at their real battle lines, there was decoy activity at other sites further from the city, on the Mousehold slopes above the Wensum, and the flat fields near the Boom Towers.

The rebels marched in the very early hours of Tuesday the 27th August. It was as well they knew the ground, as they had to find their way and work on ground still shadowed by Mousehold Heights. Not until enough light shone upon the slopes of Magdalen Hill would Kett's preparations be apparent to Warwick's observers. Once Kett's battle lines were known, Warwick had little time to properly plan the best tactics for his soldiers. It must have been clear to him then that the rebel leaders were setting the pace, and he faced some other troubling facts; the rebels had the field artillery captured from his own men; he could not be sure if Kett's army outnumbered his total fighting force; and his choices of exit from the city were severely limited. He could not sensibly use Magdalen or Pockthorpe gates, and even St. Augustine's gate was dangerously close to the rebels' high ground. His only safe exit was through St. Martin's-at-Oak.*

He first marshalled his foot soldiers in an area beside the Coslany Gate, called Justin's acre. (The 'Jousting Field' of earlier times.) Then, having marched out of the city, the battle lines to which Kett's choice of battle site had committed them, were close. Where Warwick's men were then arranged in their battle positions, in the valley area marked by what we now call Waterloo Road, they faced the rebels; they also faced the morning sun. The rebels' battle lines overlooked that valley, but they faced away from the sun, so they could see their enemy with perfect clarity. The rebels also had a southward view over the city, where Magdalen Hill slopes down to the city wall beside Bull Close, making it a dangerous funnel for Warwick's men to enter. Rebels had broken through the wall there two days before. If victorious in their last battle, that breach in the wall would have been used again for a mass re-entrance to the city. Perhaps that previous attack on Sunday the 25th had been a rehearsal or practical test.

While some rebels dug-in their defensive line of stakes, others threw up earthworks, probably over what we now know as Sprowston Road, at its junction with Magdalen and Northcote Roads; at 'Point House', as it was later known. There it would effectively block a flanking action onto the northwest slopes of Magdalen Hill. And yet, we are told, one of Warwick's captains did indeed lead such an action. Was it over the earthworks, or through that dangerous funnel along Bull Close Road? Whichever it was, it was a brave action, and must have marked a decisive point in the battle. The fortunes of conflict wavered on both sides for several hours, until the rebels realised they were losing.

---

* Then known as Cosn'y Gate, Cosn'y being an abbreviation of Coslany.

The Rebel Route to Battle

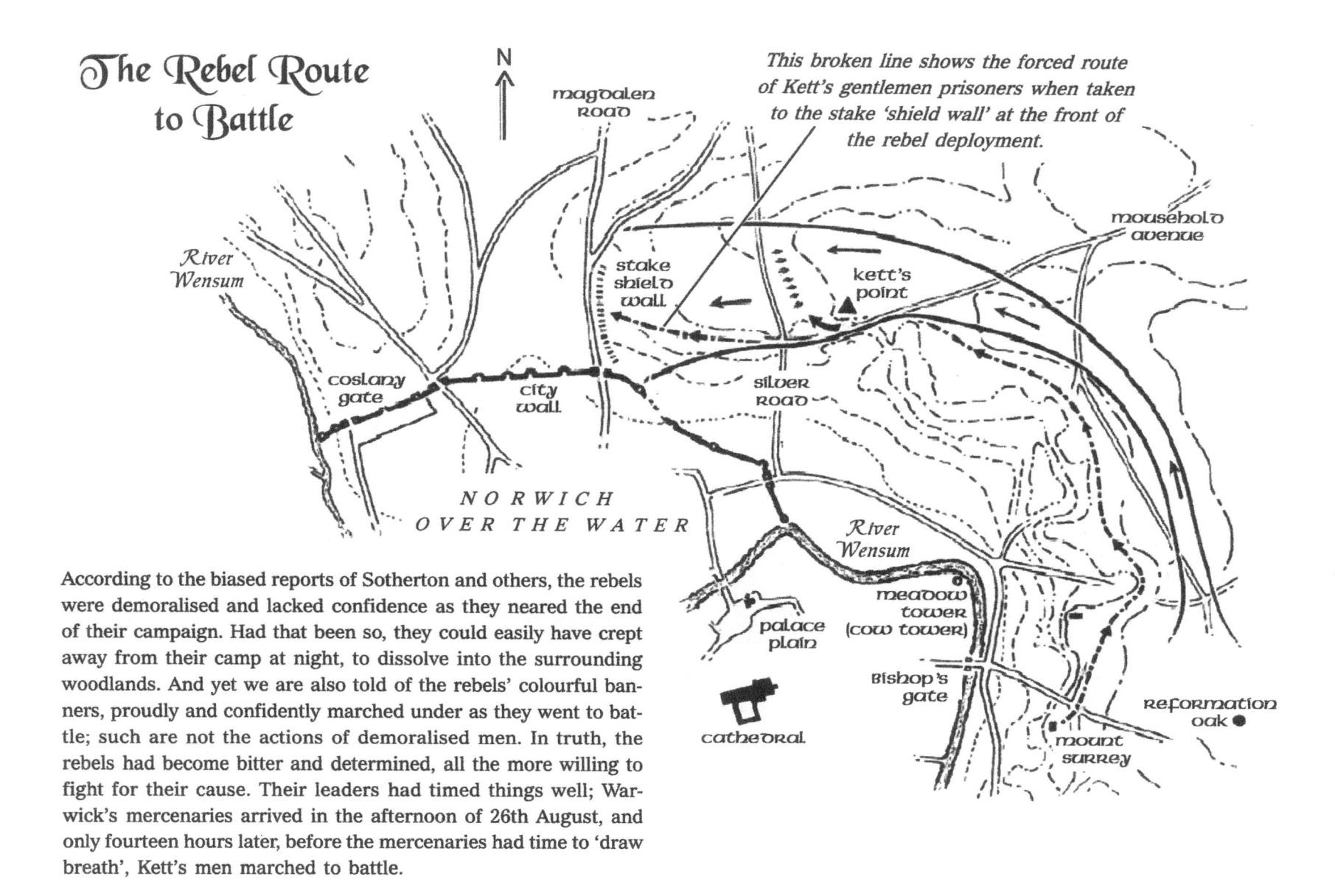

This broken line shows the forced route of Kett's gentlemen prisoners when taken to the stake 'shield wall' at the front of the rebel deployment.

According to the biased reports of Sotherton and others, the rebels were demoralised and lacked confidence as they neared the end of their campaign. Had that been so, they could easily have crept away from their camp at night, to dissolve into the surrounding woodlands. And yet we are also told of the rebels' colourful banners, proudly and confidently marched under as they went to battle; such are not the actions of demoralised men. In truth, the rebels had become bitter and determined, all the more willing to fight for their cause. Their leaders had timed things well; Warwick's mercenaries arrived in the afternoon of 26th August, and only fourteen hours later, before the mercenaries had time to 'draw breath', Kett's men marched to battle.

The view from Kett's Point

The main battle area was to the right of this view.

Kett's Point, the grassy knoll beside Mousehold Lane. Some bushes have been airbrushed out to 'open' the view.

'Kett's Point' is on the spur of land projecting westward from Mousehold. There Kett and his leading rebels had this view of the city and the North Wall. The knoll was higher and steeper in Kett's time, but possibly re-shaped somewhat in recent times during the building of an adjacent housing estate.

1. Kett's Cave; hidden from view.
2. River Wensum.
3. Pockthorpe (or Barr) Gate.
4. The Polygonal Tower on Silver Road.
5. The breach in the wall at Bull Close.
6. Cosn'y Gate and 'Justin's Acre'.

Visible on the horizon are the Cathedral, the Castle, and St. Giles' church.

On Magdalen Hill, Battle Day

The Morning of August 27th

In the very early hours of the morning, two hundred rebels dug-in the rows of 'shield wall' stakes, their defensive front lines. The rows of stakes curved round the lower westward facing slope of the hill, close to the bend of Magdalen Road, in an arc of about 1000 feet. They were spaced one yard apart, in one or two rows. Up to 50 men had cut and shaped these 300 to 500 stakes over many days. Some may have been stored earlier in hideouts such as 'Kett's Cave', close to the battle site. A similar work force cut trenches, while armed men stood ready to protect them.

Kett's guns and supply waggons rolled along the gentler slope of track we call Mousehold Avenue, and turned onto the gun-flat, now Crome Road. (It included part of the grounds of what is now the George White Middle School.) The guns were made ready.

When the early morning light bathed the slopes of Magdalen Hill, the reality of Kett's strong battle lines became apparent. Alerted, the Earl had only the Cosn'y Gate through which to lead his men to meet the rebels, his safest and only practical route to battle. By then Kett's foot soldiers, under twenty war banners, had already advanced down the broad front of Magdalen Hill.

In this down hill view from Kett's point, we see Warwick's army as small dots in the distance moving into position. By then the rebel foot soldiers were almost ready, and their gun crews were at their stations on the gun 'flat'. From Kett's Point, the rebel leaders could see into the city, the full curve of the northern city wall with its ruined North Wall Gates, and all the way over the valley floor (now Waterloo and Heath Roads) to Warwick's battle lines.

On the Field of Battle

The presence of the entire rebel force so close to the North Wall awakened the civic authorities and Warwick to the possibility of another rebel invasion. If Warwick had not promptly responded to Kett's obvious challenge to come out and do battle, the rebels could have changed the aim of their guns to blast more openings in the North Wall, enabling them to stream en-mass towards the city centre. More than that, the civic leaders no doubt feared a bombardment of the city itself, aimed first at Warwick's camp in the market square as the prelude to another invasion.

See the dispositions diagram, page 32

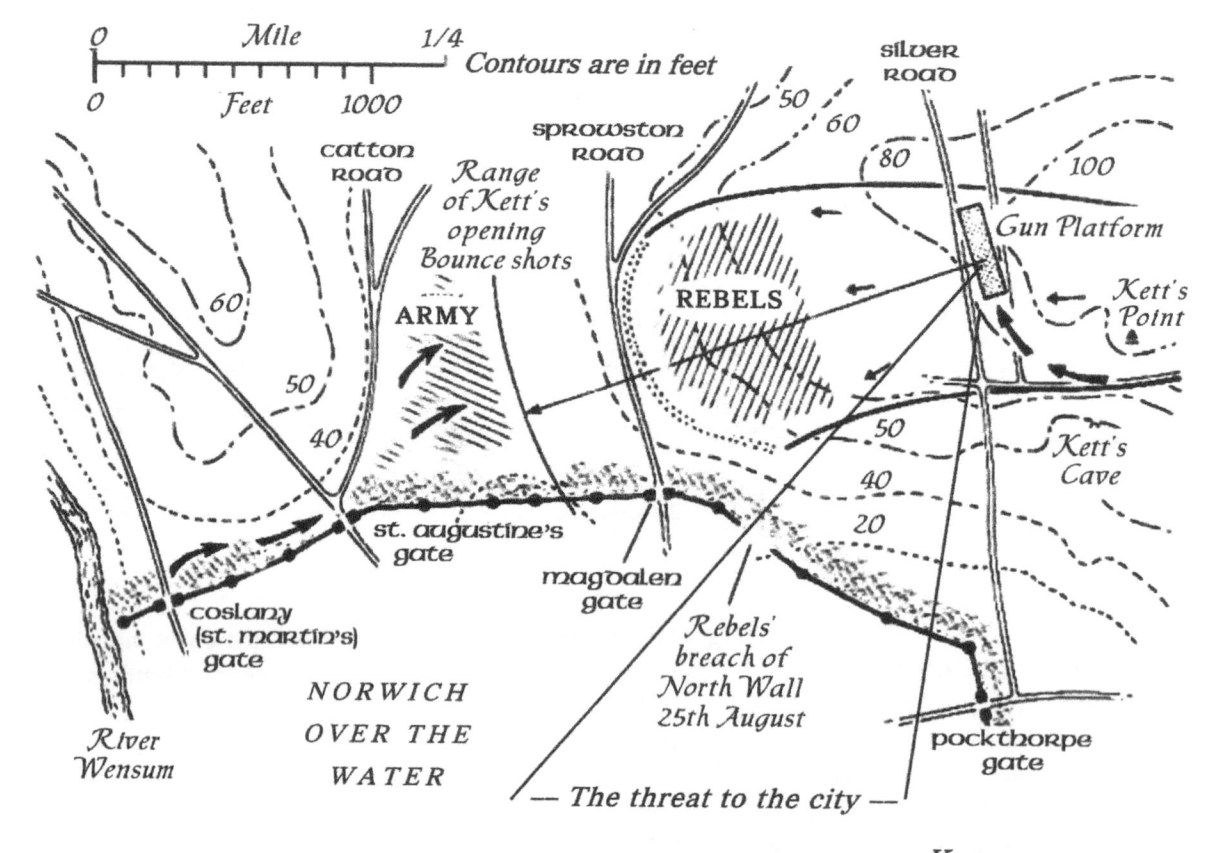

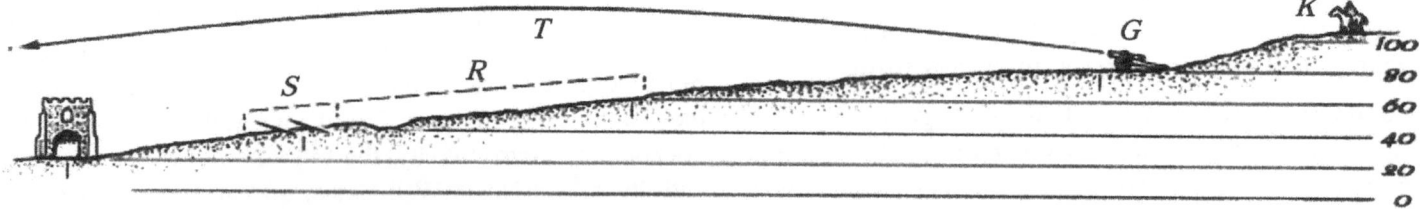

— The threat to the city —

A cross section of Magdalen Hill, showing rebel positions including 'Kett's Point' at K. G: Gun Platform. T: Typical trajectory of saker shots. S: Stake shield wall. R: Rebel deployment.

Height in feet.

The Battle

According to Nicholas Sotherton, Warwick was prompted by kindness when once more offering pardons to the rebels. In reality he may have had in mind what worried Thomas Howard, the Earl of Surrey, while preparing for the 1513 battle at Flodden. In a message to the Scottish King James IV., Howard noted that the King's men were on rising ground, arranged 'like a fortress'.

> *"So would the King please bring his men down, to fight on a level field?"*

Of course, the King declined. Thirty six years later, John Dudley, the Earl of Warwick, faced a similar problem. Knowing Kett's rebels would not descend from their superior position on Magdalen Hill, his offer of pardons, if accepted, would have been the answer to his dilemma. As we know, the rebels did not oblige.

Some writers have said that Kett was wrong to give up his high ground advantage by leaving Mousehold; but Kett and Miles viewed it differently. Although then on the relatively lower ground, the steep slope of Magdalen Hill still gave the rebels an enormous advantage over Warwick's positions on the lower ground.

Kett and Miles had wisely supposed that their best chance of success lay in prompting the battle speedily, before Warwick's Landsknechtes had time to fully recover from their long forced march, and before their own force was diminished by desertions.

Then, as planned, Kett's first troops to descend the hill were his horse soldiers with ribbons in their hats, bearing twenty battle banners and captured lances. Next came the ammunition carts, supply wagons and his many cannons. The supply waggons stopped at the crest of Magdalen Hill, near Kett's point.

A little further down, the cannons and ammunition carts turned onto the flat below the crest (now Crome Road) and immediately prepared for action. The foot soldiers flowed down the slopes and, with the horse soldiers, arranged themselves for battle. At the crest of the hill the supply waggons were quickly off loaded, rolled half way down the hill, formed into a line parallel to the stake shield wall and turned on their sides. They were to be a defensive barrier for the thousands of archers who formed up behind them. From these somewhat safer positions, the archers could launch their rain of arrows in steep trajectories.

The rebels were ready at an early hour, facing westward away from the morning sun. Warwick learned early of the rebel deployment and was not slow to respond. Most of his foot soldiers first assembled on the land long known as Justin's Acre, almost certainly the field used of old for jousting sports and military exercises. First to pass under the arch of Cosn'y (Coslany) Gate were his mounted men, then the pikemen, then the main mass of his troops. At the battle lines, Warwick's assembly was more traditional, with ranks of arquebusiers at the front, backed by mounted knights and nobles, and behind them his best foot soldiers, and most of the mercenaries. At the flanks were whatever cannons Warwick was able to muster. Warwick's entire force were obliged to face eastward into the full glare of the morning sun.

According to one of the chronicles, Warwick kept his English soldiers out of the battle, so that they should not face 'their own kind' in open combat. In truth, he needed to keep a back-up reserve close at hand in the city.

The fighting men of both armies could not have wanted any delay of the start of battle; and a good general does not stand his men ready for battle then keep them waiting. Delays add to battle fears, so the rule must be 'march, deploy, fight'.

Blomefield and other writers simplistically described Warwick's order of battle as follows; cannons were fired to 'soften up' the rebel lines; arquebusiers fired volleys; pikes advanced, the cavalry charged, the rebels fled in disorder.

Had it been so simple, the battle would have been over in a very short time. It began early and ended at four in the afternoon, some seven hours later, which does not suggest the immediate rout of the rebels as popularly believed. In fact it was a three part battle; the first part lasting several hours, during which time Warwick had to repeat his orders, and often command a re-grouping of his men. It was common in such battles for both sides to recognise the need for humane breaks in the fighting, for the removal of the dead and injured, and perhaps some careful and discreet recovery of weapons while battle commanders reviewed their positions. While Kett had hundreds of battle experienced ex-navy and army personnel, realistically he did not have commanders of sufficient rank, essential for the command of cavalry, and the control of pikemen assembled into pike blocks. For the want of suitable commanders, the rebels probably did not use pikes in a highly organised manner. Against them the rebels had to face Captain Drury's repeated cavalry advances, the thrusting forward of at least two of Warwick's own pike blocks, and their new enemy, the well trained, battle hardened Dutch and German mercenaries, the Landsknechts. They were a fighting force vastly different to the Spanish and Italians used in the government army under the Marquis of Northampton; but in the rebels' minds, they were not expected to be so different to the men they had beaten before. Rather than lacking confidence, the rebels were over confident. Against that, experience and training enabled the mercenaries and cavalry to slowly but surely wear the rebels down.

Some historians have said that the outcome of the battle 'was never in doubt'; that Kett's men were easily and quickly beaten, but how can that be? By nine in the morning the battle had begun; it did not end until four in the afternoon. That is hardly a rout. Warwick's son Ambrose was there with the loyalist army, and he was not sure at the time who would be victorious. He later said that the rebel archers showed superiority over the loyalist soldiers. It is known that Ambrose favoured the longbow. For this battle his father did not, and yet Ambrose had seen the rebels' repeated hails of arrows *'decimating his father's foot soldiers and pikemen'*. In his overview of the battle, Ambrose recalled –

'The battle was so manfully fought on both sides, it could hardly be judged which side was likely to prevail.'

Which begs the question about how many loyalist troops were lost in the battle. Officially it was only about seventy men; and yet we have those words from Ambrose telling of the decimation of his father's troops, and of a battle so manfully fought it was hard to say which side would prevail. We should consider too the seven hour duration of the battle. That is a long time for so many men to survive the fierce onslaught, and here again we see reason enough for the chroniclers to be less than truthful.

Kett's Flight to Swannington

We come now to the moment the rebel lines were finally broken, and during that last hour the fast, chilling, barbarous pursuit of the fleeing rebels by Landsknechts and loyalist knights. As that devastating final onslaught began, Robert and William Kett had seen the tide of battle turning against them. With six other rebels, they fled the field, for which the chroniclers branded them cowards.

If we feel strong enough to so describe men who have faced the horrors of the battlefield and weaken at last, we should be very sure of our own possible conduct in the same circumstances. It is a fact that a man can be acclaimed a hero for facing up to one sort of danger, while in another quite different threat that same man may turn and run. Remember then the words of Walter Rye, about Kett bravely facing his own execution. It may be that what Kett dreaded was seeing the end of the campaign he and his followers had thought of as noble – which indeed it was.

While his brother William fled in the direction of his Wymondham home, rather foolishly you may think, Robert rode to the north for some miles to the village of Swannington. By going to the north, he was certainly not heading homeward. It may be that he had a vague notion of getting to the coast with the possibility of escaping abroad. Regarding the end of his desperate ride, the chronicles seem clear about events at the farm where he stopped. While in his captor's farmhouse, he choose to stay there, partly to ensure the safety of a child left with him while the farmer's wife went to the church to find her husband.

Having rested a little while, Kett could at that moment have continued with his escape before the farm-wife returned. But he did not, supposing no doubt that going on would merely delay the inevitable; and surely his horse had been securely stabled by then, by his captors, so was no longer available. The farm wife returned shortly, from which we may assume that the church in question was nearby St. Margaret's, still there in the middle of the village of Swannington.

The distance he rode late that fateful afternoon was variously stated in the chronicles, as seven or eight miles. Even though those writers were clearly dishonest in many of their statements, they had no reason to distort that part of the story, and it seems reasonable to suppose they knew not only the distance Kett rode, but also his starting point. Again, such 'gentlemen' were experienced enough to assess distances; and this should tell us something about the location of the battle ground.* The farm where Kett eventually stopped was on the edge of the village, most probably in a meadow near Church Lane. The distance given was measured from Kett's starting point on the battle ground, which gives us a reasonable estimate of up to eight miles – if we agree that the battle was at Magdalen Hill.

See page 42 and PART FOUR, page 43.

Other Supposed Battle Sites

Denmark Farm

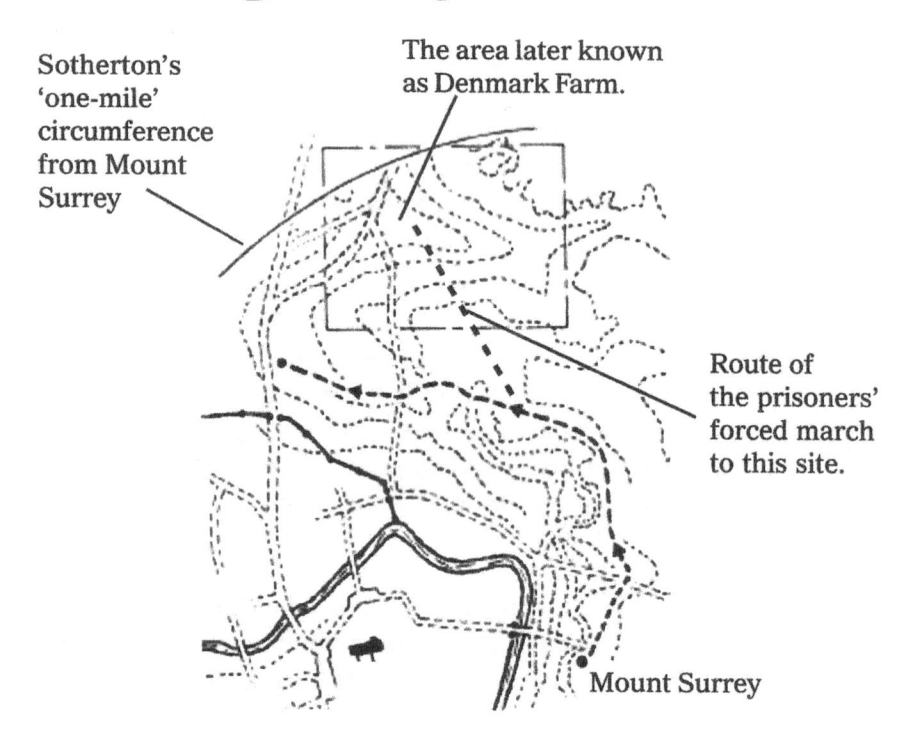

Sotherton's 'one-mile' circumference from Mount Surrey

The area later known as Denmark Farm.

Route of the prisoners' forced march to this site.

Mount Surrey

A possible battle site suggested by some earlier researchers. It would have had distinct disadvantages compared to the Magdalen Hill site, having a much reduced line of sight to the North Wall. Command communications would have been difficult.

Dussing's Deale

A field some distance to the east of Norwich, beside the road called Green Lane North has been named as the site of that final battle. It is a long way from Kett's Camp at Mount Surrey to Green Lane North, and the land between was far from flat and featureless in those days. It would have been a difficult and dangerous terrain for heavily equipped armies marching with some urgency.

There is a theory that the rebel army fled to the east, and were pursued there by Warwick's forces. However, it is most unlikely that Warwick would command his men to pursue them to such a remote location, so far from his relatively secure position in the city. For the same reason, Kett would not have ordered his rebels to march so far to the east.

PART FOUR

A full analysis of the Dussing's Deale scenario

- Compared with Magdalen Hill
- Doles and Deales • The Lumners and the Dussing's
- * Ground Surveys

The practical problems of the 'Dussindale' location in comparison with Kett's strategically ideal site at Magdalen Hill

The points against 'Dussindale' are summarised on the right, with detailed examinations on the following pages.

1. The rebels' 18 cannons and their supply waggons would have been a great burden for men and horses to haul over the rough terrain on the way to the so called 'Dussindale'.

2. Warwick's men left the city through the gate we know as St. Martins-at-Oak, the Cosney Gate. If it were true that the rebels were marching to a battleground to the east, Warwick would have used an easterly gate, such as Pockthorpe (Barr Gate) or the Bishop's Gate, these being more directly connected to easterly routes over Mousehold.

3. While following the rebels, Warwick's men would be open to ambush and would have faced the same risks along the riverside road beside the much indented steep slopes. By any other route, first to the north and then eastward, they would have had a very long trek, with similar logistical problems.

4. Warwick's reserves remaining in the city centre would be too remote from 'Dussindale' to serve as a rapid response force. Similarly, Kett would not have left men at Bull Close; it is unlikely they would remain there, being so close to Warwick's reserves.

5. Even the timescale of events tells us that the so called 'Dussindale' location was impractical. Such a mass movement of men and their battle equipment over that distance would have delayed the start of the battle to a time much later than is generally believed. Practical military sense suggests an early start to the battle.

6. If the rebels were to flee in fear of ultimate defeat, they could have dispersed at night, over country they knew well. Most would have been hard to later identify; only their leaders and about a dozen other men were well known. They could have made their way to the coast. Rebels intent on escape would certainly not leave as an assembled army, and they would not make a show of burning their camp. What the rebels had in mind was not flight, but fight.

7. The distance given for Kett's flight to Swannington, measured from his starting point on the battleground to the farm where he stopped, was reported to be about eight miles. That could only be possible if the battleground was at Magdalen Hill and Catton Vale. If we suppose instead that the battle was near Postwick, the so called 'Dussindale', then Kett would have trekked for over thirteen miles (along the Reepham Road and what is now the A1042).

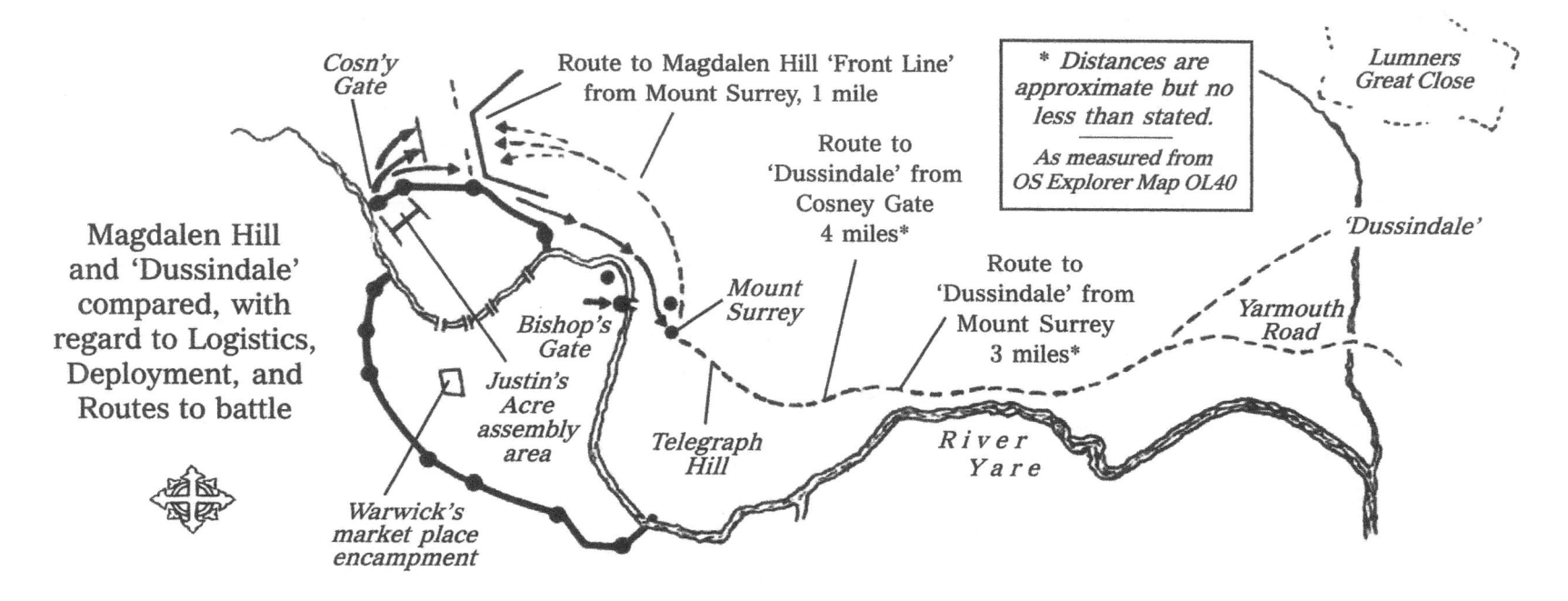

Magdalen Hill and 'Dussindale' compared, with regard to Logistics, Deployment, and Routes to battle

Cosn'y Gate

Route to Magdalen Hill 'Front Line' from Mount Surrey, 1 mile

Route to 'Dussindale' from Cosney Gate 4 miles*

Mount Surrey

Route to 'Dussindale' from Mount Surrey 3 miles*

Bishop's Gate

Justin's Acre assembly area

Telegraph Hill

Warwick's market place encampment

River Yare

Yarmouth Road

'Dussindale'

Lumners Great Close

* Distances are approximate but no less than stated.

As measured from OS Explorer Map OL40

Although it is true that Kett's men came to know the entire Mousehold area intimately, even for them the course to the supposed Dussindale would have been difficult, especially in the hours before dawn, but more so for Warwick's forces. Even when marching in daylight, they had less knowledge of the terrain. All of which amounts to a great deal of effort by both sides so soon before a battle. Men heavily laden might not march faster than five miles an hour; in all probability, slower than that over difficult terrain. (Roman records tell of a marching pace of 24 miles in 8 hours.) With horses hauling heavy artillery, it was a demanding deployment of forces in a short period of time. Most historians accept that the final conflict began at an early hour. Kett wanted to wrong-foot Warwick, and cause his mercenaries to be called into action too soon after their arrival. 'Dussings Deale' was far too remote for that ploy.

The indictments of Robert Kett and his brother state that their 'treachery' was in the parishes of Thorpe and Sprowston. The rebel camp was in Thorpe; and the area to the northeast of the northern city wall was part of Sprowston. The extensive Thorpe Parish referred to in the indictments against the Ketts, does have an eastern boundary close to the Plumstead Parish and the Dussings Deale site. It is argued that, through that close proximity, the indictments may have been in error; but such an error is highly unlikely. Boundaries of personal property and parishes were so often a cause for contention that misrepresentations were promptly challenged. Citizens were proud and jealous of their parishes, and parish lines had to be just as carefully defined as the property boundaries influenced by them. When judging this case of treachery, the court needed to be precise in all such details.

It has been suggested that both rebel and loyalist forces used the 'Old Yarmouth Road', which goes over part of the heath, on what we know as Telegraph Lane. Such a course would not be easy going for heavily laden men and animals. Neither was there a smooth road for an ascent up to the summit of the Mousehold plateaux in those days and such roads were not well maintained, there being scouring and subsidence from poorly controlled drainage off the higher slopes of the plateaux. For the loyalists there was the added danger of passing beside wooded country ideal for snipers; none of this being a welcome prelude to battle. While it is obviously true that Warwick's troops knew how to undertake long treks, such as their march from Cambridge to Norwich, such treks were well planned and organised on roads better known than those used for such an impromptu march to 'Dussindale.' Such a march by the rebels would have been time consuming, leaving fewer hours for battle preparations. For the loyalists, leaving the city by the Cosny Gate and marching the greater distance of over four miles, there would have had even less preparation time. If the loyalists had made such a march, then went immediately into battle, Sotherton, so intent on offering Warwick and his troops the utmost praise, would have grandly heralded it in his narrative. Instead, we are merely told that Warwick's troops passed out of Cosny gate and marched to battle. Absence of such acclaim is clear evidence that the four mile trek to the supposed Dussindale site did not happen, and that both sides prepared for a battle much closer to the city and the rebel camp.

It is probably true that Robert Kett decided to face Warwick on the battle field before the number of his own troops was too much reduced by desertions. That being so, how strange it would have been for him to lead his men to a battle site so remote that it would be much easier for them to desert; not only at the battle site, but on the three mile rough country trek leading to it. Having deserted at 'Dussindale', an escape to the north and east may have been so easy. The rebels wore no uniforms, and could merge into the surrounding country, looking for sympathetic country folk to help them.

It is also doubtful that Warwick would lead his army so far from the city, leaving only his foot soldiers there to keep order, in itself a dubious task; and they could hardly stand ready as a 'rapid response' force to support the main force at a battle site more than four miles away. It is also hard to understand why Warwick would lead his men out of the city by the Cosny Gate for the start of a long march to the so called Dussindale, when departure through the Bishop's Gate would be much more direct. It is argued that rebels were in that area, standing between the loyalist troops and the gate; but that would be most unlikely if it were also true that all other men of the rebel force had left to prepare a battle site far to the east at 'Dussindale'. Kett would not leave men in the city, so cut off from his main force, and so close to the attentions of Warwick's reserve troops. Rebels left behind could serve little purpose. It is argued that the other North Wall gates were too damaged for Warwick's men to pass through; and yet Cosn'y Gate, the gate Warwick used, had also been heavily targeted by the rebels; and there was also a passable route through the breach the rebels had made in the North Wall two days earlier. In fact, Warwick used the Cosny Gate because it was furthest from the committed battle area. Alexander Neville had something surprisingly informative to say about that.

Describing Warwick's men passing out of Cosn'y Gate, Neville tells us they were *'Marching directly against the enemy...'* According to Raphael Holinshed, one of the writers of a voluminous history, Warwick and his army *'issued forth from the city, marching straight towards the enemy'*, and saw the rebels in *'rudimentary formation'* on rising ground. It was sensible for Warwick to accept the challenge of a battle site close by; he had reserves close at hand in the city, patrolling the narrow city streets and on station in the market square. It was also sensible of Kett to keep a force of his own within the city walls at Bull Close. Kett decided to stage the last battle as soon as possible, allowing the newly arrived mercenaries little time to draw breath. He and Miles would have planned far ahead for the deployment of their men and materials onto the slopes of Magdalen Hill. The rebels, true to their cause, marched from their Mousehold camp as an assembled and well equipped army, having made a show of defiance by demolishing and burning their camp at night. That act was, as we would say these days, 'a statement' for all to see, by the glowing fires and towering palls of smoke.

It is interesting that none of the early writers mention the actual distance marched by the Earl's troops after passing out of the Cosny Gate; neither do they name the battle site in the usual way with a title based on its locality. That seems strange until we accept that highly placed persons could have commanded that there must be no mention of it. Kett's rebels brazenly bringing the battle to the doors of the city would have been an act too humiliating for the Earl of Warwick, and dangerous for him if its significance was understood by rival members of the Privy Council; Warwick had made too many mistakes on this campaign. Doing nothing to prevent the rebels from challenging him so close to the city would have been seen as another failure.

If the rebels did put their faith in a prophesy about 'Dussindale', did any of them have certain knowledge of its location? Or that it still or ever existed, if based on nothing more than a local memory of another place or a long ago event. We should be mindful of soldiers in the last century singing of places many of them knew little about; *'Its a Long Way to Tipperary'* and *'The Road to Mandalay'* were simply good marching songs. Kett's men may have put a tune to their prophesied 'Dussindale'.

It has been suggested that the water course seen on the Bryant and Faden maps (page 42) flowed through a valley deep enough to become the mass burial site of battle dead and their armament. Some memories of such burials tend to be handed down the generations. There seems to be no such folklore about it in nearby Postwick and Plumstead. In reality, the water course was probably filled in some time in the intervening centuries, not to bury men, but to extend useful areas of arable or grazing land.

There must be undetected mass graves somewhere, possibly under the vast expanse of Mousehold in some of the big gravel scrapes, of which there were many; or possibly under houses and thoroughfares of the real battle area. A resident of the area, who may not be named, has described his dark sensations when walking in the Silver Road / Mousehold Lane area. If the generations of his family have long resided there, extending far enough back through the centuries, there may well have been implanted a hereditary memory of the sad end to the valiantly fought final battle of Kett's rebellion.

Doles and Deales...

The Plumstead Parish map of 1718, it being a Chapter Estate map, is clearly concerned only with estate boundaries, and shows only one interesting physical feature, 'The Great Old Dyke,' and that only because it formed part of an estate boundary. It does not even show or name the Gargytt Hills. Although the map as drawn is the result of poor surveying, we may be sure its authors clearly understood its intended purpose. The name of one estate ownership dominates the map; Lumner's. Another name, stated here with the spelling as seen on the map is *Dussings,* and that with the full estate title *'Dussings Deale.'* By the use of the word Deale, a parcel of land was clearly referred to. It was conveniently associated with a sheep walk, hence the full annotation on the map being 'Dussings Deale & Postwick sheep walk.' Note that it does not read 'OR Postwick sheep walk' as has been misread. The ampersand tells us the sheep walk was *not* an alternative name for the Dussings Deale plot, but of its dual purpose. Of course, the word deale is synonymous with dole, the latter being the preferred word when the survey map of 1589 was prepared, so on that map we see its frequent use. Significantly, that same map does show, on its western end, features to do with the rebellion, such as Kett's Reformation Oak and Thorpe Wood. There is no mention on that map of a battle site at the other end of the map near Little Lumners.

The interpretation of 'Dussings Deale' as 'Dussindale' is clearly inappropriate. There are place names similar to 'Dussindale' mentioned in other documents, but none offer us a locality. There are no maps seen so far that show such a place, and nothing similar to it clearly marking a historic site.

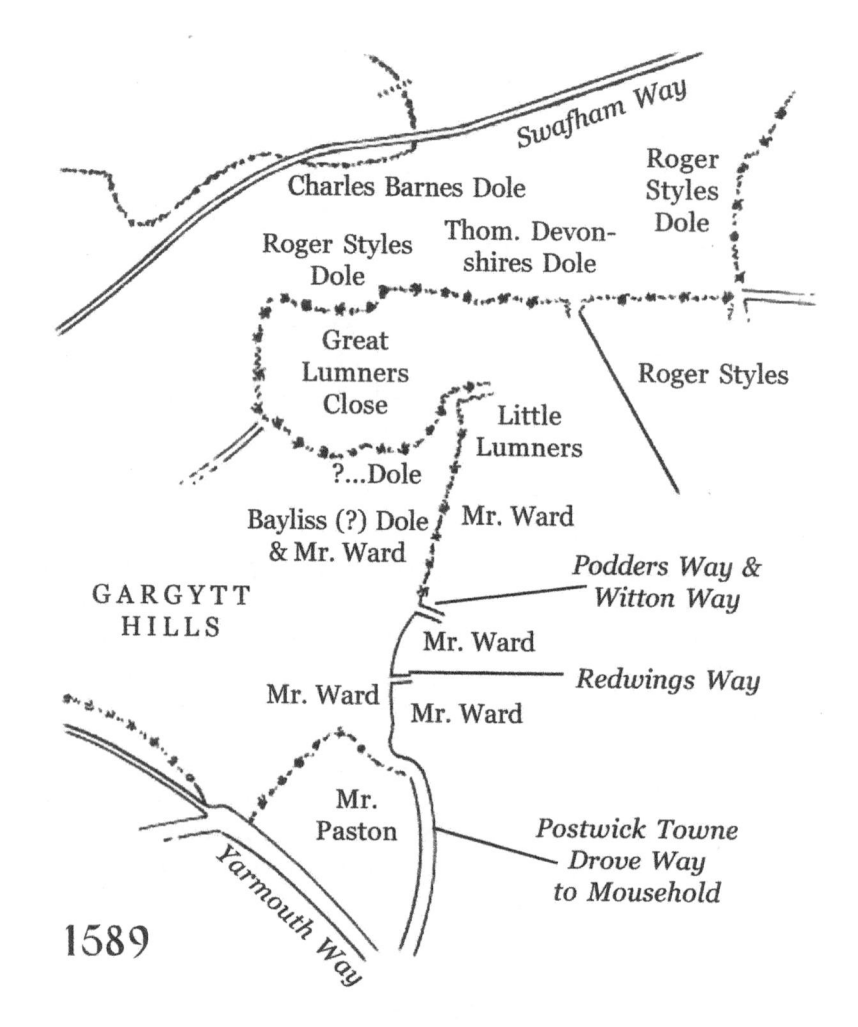

Above. A section of the 1589 map, redrawn and re-annotated. It shows the emphasis on persons and their Doles. Mr. Ward's presence proves the absence of Dussing's there at that time. Perhaps the Dussing's had a Deale somewhere else, as yet unidentified.

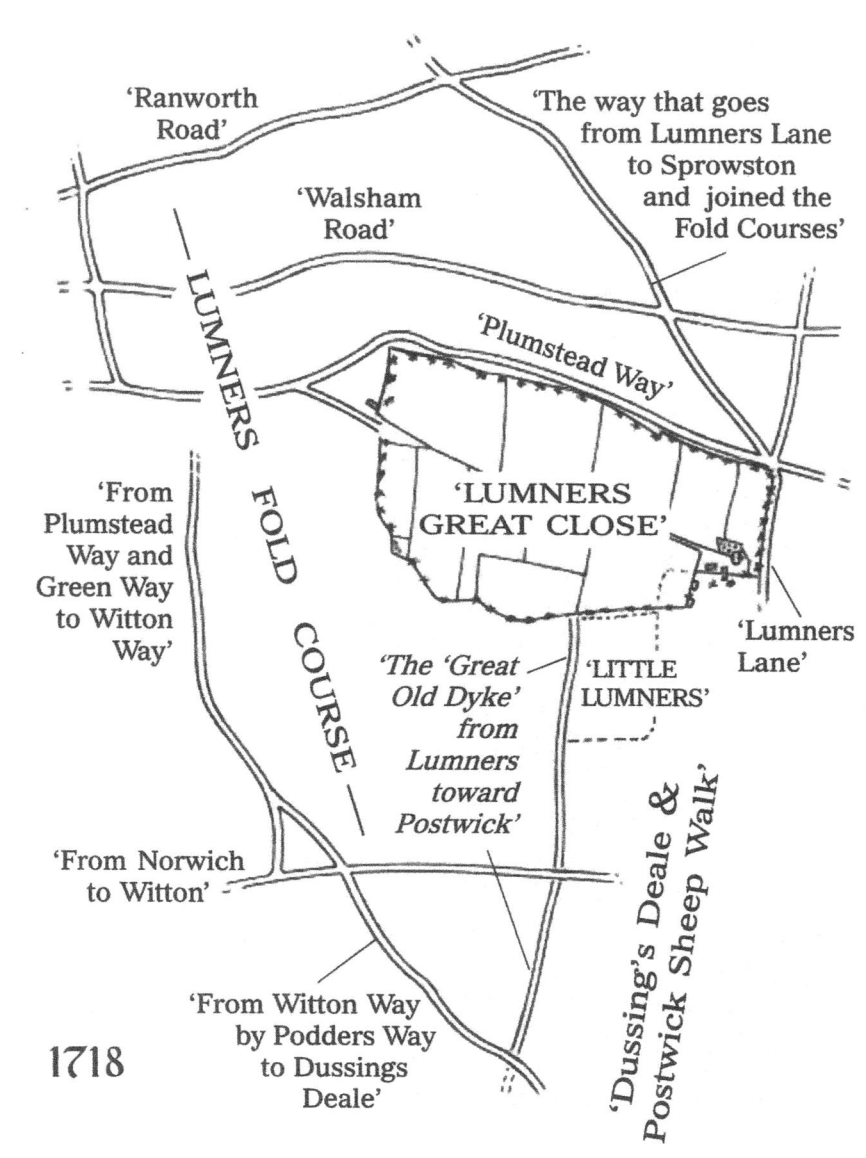

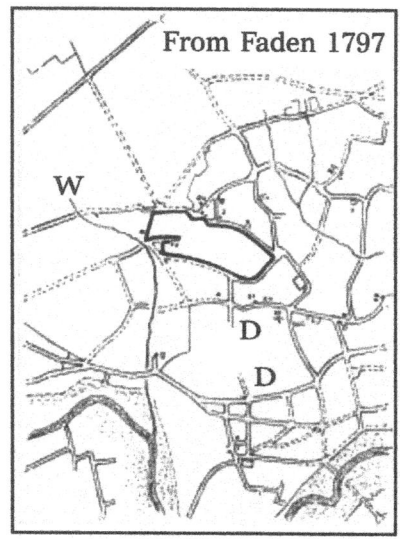

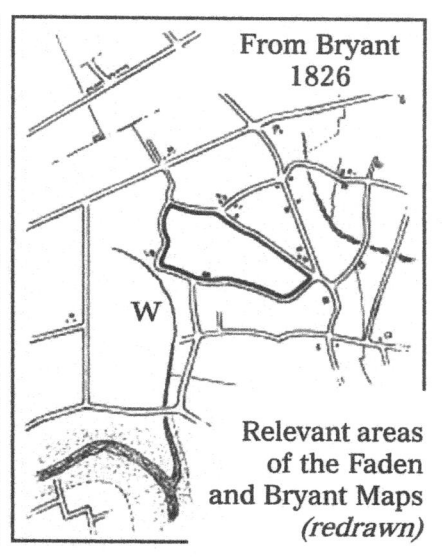

Left; a redrawn detail from the Plumstead Parish Estates map of 1718. The original survey, being so poorly set out, does not easily relate to the later maps by Faden and Bryant, above. To help with recognition, I have heavily outlined the approximate position and area of Lumners Great Close. Note that on these maps the water course (W) is clearly visible. It is hard to believe that the reference to a 'Great Old Dyke' on the 1718 map, its line being so straight and its course so oddly placed, could possibly refer to the same water course. It may instead refer to a 'Dyke' in the Dutch sense; a long embankment *'from Lumners toward Postwick'* raised up as a strong boundary between Lumner's Fold Course and Dussing's Deale. We should note that the caption reads *'toward Postwick'*, not *to the River Yare*. Although later ploughed out, remnants of the dyke may be what is indicated on the Faden map at (D). The actual water course (W) on these later maps is clearly shown flowing all the way down to the River Yare.

The Lumners and the Dussings

There is significant information at the Public Record Office in Norwich regarding the names of relevant land owners or tenants. On the lists of their published wills, two such names appear on the map of the Plumstead Parish; Lumners and Dussing.

The surname Dussing, with a spelling as seen on the map, is a family name with representation elsewhere in Norfolk. From a list of wills we first see it in the year 1465. Others of that name were typically from Kyrkeby Bydon, Kyrkeby St. Andrew, of a parson of Burnham Thorpe and Erpingham. The last entry is from the year 1668-69. Dussing and its variations were words associated with the North Sea timber trade, probably from the days of Hanseatic trading. It mainly regarded quantities of cut timber rather than types of it; in Sweden, dussin means a dozen. Dussing was common in Germany, and also well known in Austria. It is also seen with the spelling Dussyng. Dussin without the 'g' was common in Italy and France. Duffin is a variation or misspelling, possibly from a misunderstanding of the double 'ss' which in cursive script looks like a double ff. It first appears in will lists of 1662, the last entry is for 1824. Another variation, Duffing's, is listed from 1494 to 1527. Duffin's are listed in telephone directories. This wide spread use of the name suggests the possibility of other *Dussing's* with 'deales' or 'doles' elsewhere in the county.

The local use of the name Lumner first appears on a will list of 1581, for Diams Lumner from Tuttington. There followed Elizabeth Lumner of Norwich in 1591, Frances Lumner of East Dereham in 1690 and Mary, probably a Lumner, from Wells.

Ground Surveys

Ground survey devices have been used by a Leeds University Research Team, for a digital terrain analysis of the Dussings Deale area. This, with their 'map regression' studies, provided some interesting new knowledge of the landscape in previous centuries. Wherever and however used, the technique constitutes a useful research tool, and some of the results for this site could be of interest to students of local Holocene period geology.

For historians, some of the topographical features found would suit certain requirements of a chosen battlefield, but so too would many other sites with a similar terrain. As admitted in the research report, *'map regression is not an exact science.'* The report also admits that *'The resultant composite maps will always contain an element of uncertainty'* and *'The results cannot be regarded as completely definitive.'* Even though the results of the work revealed no proof of an actual battle site, merely that the regression-revealed landscape was suitable for it, an imaginative scenario was written describing battle tactics.

Metal detectorists worked over the area before building foundations were laid. We are told the instruments were inadvertently set at a level too low to respond to lead, even though lead, in the form of firearms shot, is the very evidence detectorists should look for in a historic battle site. However, lead shot survives in the ground for a long time, far longer than the ferrous metals of arrowheads and bolts; so at such sites there could be enough lead en-mass to register its presence even with the instrument set at such an inappropriate level.

PART FIVE

Robert Kett

• The man, his conscience and his cause • The Reformation Oak
• Chronicles of Deception • Walk where the Rebels Marched to Battle

Robert Kett, a pillar of Wymondham society, was law abiding, successful in business, with much comfort to look forward to through the later years of his life; he has been called a most improbable rebel. It could simply be that this seemingly enigmatic man was a caring soul who became increasingly aware of the growing number of dispossessed people, the unjust treatment of the poor, and the harsh attitudes of those who cared only for their own wealth. Perhaps a glowing light of selfless reason came to him on his own road to a personal Damascus, by which he could suddenly see that the wealthy were bleeding the economy dry and reducing more and more people to poverty.

And you may think that now in our time, that all has a familiar ring to it.

Even on those fateful July days in Wymondham Kett must have realised that becoming the leader of these rebels and despised poor was a dangerous step. He seems to have been moved by the hardship and anger which had been spreading country wide for some time. There must have been so many warning stirrings of it, and yet the government were wrong footed by the suddenness of the rebellions when they came at last. Through not having enough regular soldiers the country was not militarily strong, and the government could no longer depend upon the feudal knights and their private armies. No doubt other would-be rebel leaders throughout the England of 1549, all awaiting the right moment, had hoped the time had come to show their hands. Only six of England's counties had no such underlying discontent.

Many historians have long argued that there could have been no links between the troubles in the West of England and events here in Norfolk, the understanding being that it was Archbishop Cranmer's new English prayer book that finally upset the people of Devon and Cornwall, whereas here the problems were purely economic, as if the citizens of Eastern England had simply accepted the late King Henry's new church, in a mass turn round of faith. That is highly unlikely; the Catholic faith had for so long been embedded in people's lives, with rituals and images that pleased the majority. Kett himself had as a youth devoutly followed the strictly catholic services in the Abbey at Wymondham and would most certainly have had a part in the cherished (illegal) celebrations of the martyr Thomas Beckett in the chapel named for him. We should rightly conclude that the strife that evolved throughout the troubled English counties was born of a combination of religious and economic upsets. A potent combination, and there was little difference in motivation between the east and the west.

Blomefield, in the part he contributed to the 1806 *History of Norfolk,* seemed to have gained old knowledge of a common sympathy and a common purpose, and made much of it in the section about the rebellions:

'Devonshire and Norfolk, remote from each other, communicated councils for carrying out their design.'

There is evidence of predetermined prompting whispered here in Norfolk; it is recorded that men secretly ran 'hither and thither between Wymondham and Norwich in the days before Kett joined the rebels; and in all probability there had been messengers going from county to county, with thoughts and plans for a countrywide uprising. Note how Blomefield refers to *'...their design...'*

There is also the matter of letters discovered, which tell of previously unsuspected meetings between Kett and the Norwich Bishop William Rugge; perhaps both men were still determined Catholics and happened also to share strong social consciences. Through a suspicion that Rugge was attached to the rebels, he was threatened with prosecution for having a part in the rebellion. After the rebellion, he was removed from office. He and Kett would have been prime contacts for a nationwide action. We may wonder too how many others of the church hierarchy kept hidden their dislike of the new church order. However, it may not have been so much the loss of the Catholic faith that so upset the population, as the loss of what the monasteries had given to generations of them. In their better days, the men of Holy Orders had provided for the populace something akin to a welfare state, so much so that a man and his family in genuine poverty need not go hungry if a convent or monastery could be reached. Those were also the places where some of the brightest poor children could gain an education.

Within that care was also a medical service, and support for the elderly. There were other ways in which monasteries and related churches were special places for the poor living in grey, light-less, colourless surroundings. By welcome contrast, in the great buildings of their faith, there was the glowing light of many lamps and candles, the warmth of congregations, huge colourful wall paintings of God and the Saints, and holy iridescence from the high arched windows. All of that was swept away with the monasteries, and many men, previously employed by them, lost their livelihoods. For most there had been 'a job for life' and medicare when they needed it. For such reasons it is possible that the majority of people throughout the country had fond memories and longed for the return of all that comforting warmth, and carefully and secretly remained 'catholic' in principle if not in strongly held belief. Against that, it is certain that some places of holy order became somewhat less than holy, with monks and novices corrupting what they had inherited from their forbears, thereby giving fuel to the propaganda merchants supporting Henry's urge to dispel the power and governance of Rome.

It is hard to find reasons for only the people of the West Country remaining true to that faith. Kett's decision in July of 1549 may not after all have been so spontaneous, or entirely altruistic. Perhaps he saw the platform of rebel leadership as only his first step to something much bigger, with himself at the head of it. If the Norfolk rebels had won that last great battle, that would have been a rallying cry for the whole country. But what sort of organisations could hold the whole country together against established authority? They would need strong social bonds somewhat akin to the unions of our time. The closest to those in Kett's time were the great number and types of well organised guilds.

However, added to the guilds we must remember the most important line of support. If Bishop Rugge, with enough other like minded church leaders did want a return to Catholicism, then the Vatican, the greatest Christian force, would have been interested and tempted to become involved. Edward VI was still very young, and it may have been hoped that his head could be turned away from his father's Anglican church. Apart from that, the intensely Catholic Mary Tudor and her supporters probably contemplated her own climb to the throne, an ascent which would ensure the re-emergence of Catholicism in England. Her residence at Kenninghall was close enough to Wymondham for early contacts between her agents and a willing rebel leader, by name Robert Kett.

Henry and his government had ruled that Mary should be next in line, but Earl Warwick had his daughter-in-law Lady Jane Grey, a protestant, declared Queen ahead of Mary. It was announced in the marketplace in King's Lynn. Even though that act was quite properly challenged, Warwick could find little support, especially in Norfolk, and later Mary was crowned. For his treachery Warwick was doomed.

The rebellion was clearly driven by poverty and injustice, but religion was certainly part of it. Had the rebels won, then Kett's position as leader would have been strong indeed, especially if supported by the guilds.

Early in their campaign, the rebels believed in the support of Lord Protector Somerset, the young King's uncle, but during the rebellion Somerset was challenged by the Privy Council, and deposed by Warwick and his supporters. Warwick became the strong decisive leader of the Privy Council, and showed himself to be an *'Apostle of Force'*, and the right person to put down the rebellion, which he did despite some tactical errors. Although support for rebel action continued after 1549 up to at least 1554, some of the cruellest men were able to hold onto power. The common people had to wait a long time for the better lives and fairer government that truly great men like Robert Kett had tried to gain for them. Now we, in our time, should honour Kett, as did some survivors of the rebellion. Even before the trials of Robert and his brother William, the rebel Ralph Claxton defiantly said;

*'I did well in Mr. Kett's camp –
he trusted to see a new day for such as I.'*

In a book entitled 'The History of Norfolk' two men facing execution are compared. They are the adversaries Robert Kett, 'the Tanner of Wymondham', and John Dudley, the Earl of Warwick. From these memorable words by Walter Rye, we have this satisfying closing thought –

*'He (Kett) did not grovel for mercy..
...as did Warwick four years after...'*

For it seems that Kett went to his hanging from the keep at Norwich Castle in relative calm, while John Dudley, the Earl of Warwick, having been found guilty of treason for his attempt to change the order of the monarchy, was taken to the block at the Tower of London, begging for his life. How the wheel of fortune turns, for fate to award its own justice.

The Reformation Oak

Kett's Great Oak of Reformation could not remain standing, to live and shower its acorns for centuries to come. It had been the centre of the rebels' court and council, and they were gone; but local memories of them would live on down the ages, and the great tree could become a place of martyrdom, giving the women and children of the cruelly executed men a place to kneel and pray, as their ill fated fathers, husbands or sons had happily done when the rebellion bore a promise of success and better times. For them, the tree had become a powerful sign of their faith; a church, an altar and council chamber. No doubt mourners came to that quiet and peaceful woodland, women and ragged children still grieving and praying there annually; but the powerful men ruling England could not allow that to go on. So we may reasonably suppose that some years after the tree had known the last of the executions, the peace of the woodland floor was disturbed once more by horsemen obeying an order to look for the Great Reformation Oak, to search among the trees, and recognise it at last by the benches built round it for Kett's council meetings. Then having found it, waiting while the Marine Council shipwrights assessed the boughs that may fit their prescribed patterns; then sawyers and carpenters climbing up and cutting away the topmost branches; all the debris piling up on the woodland floor with the chopped up wooden benches, all to become fuel for city fires and ovens.

And hiding among the trees, the women who had heard news of what was happening to their tree, secretly watching and praying, while the sawyers and loggers did their work. The wide space around the great oak, where rebels had assembled, gave the men all the space they needed to work, using stout ropes, chains and pulley blocks, lowering the heavy boughs, slowly bringing the noble tree down to its stump; then gangs of prisoners from the castle, digging a wide deep hole around the stump to reveal its mass of roots, for sawyers to work on them with saws and axes, chopping and sawing for days; then teams of heavy horses hauling the mighty stump out of its hole, the hole being filled and prisoners with stout brooms sweeping away the debris until only scattered oak leaves remained, to become leaf mould, or be blown away by the gentlest breeze. The Great Oak of Reformation so totally gone that no strangers would ever believe that such a mighty and once so important tree had ever stood there; but local people knew and talked of it for generations, until even their memories of it faded. Centuries later, some local citizens would insist that the tree had stood somewhere else on Mousehold for hundreds of years more, and some remember it being taken down by order of a city council. In our time, many still debate their theories about where it once stood. But no matter; like the stories of Robert Kett, his rebels and their battles, the tree will live on in folklore.

Chronicles of Deception

'The Commoyson in Norfolk 1549'
Nicholas Sotherton, 14??–1540?

His identity is not certain, as there appears to have been more than one person of that name. He was probably related to Thomas Sotherton, the merchant-mayor who invited Fleming and Walloon refugees to Norwich to boost the local textile trade; and possibly to Leonard Sotherton who rode in haste to London to tell the Privy Council of Kett's 'invasion' of Norwich. When Nicholas wrote of the rebellion, he is said to have called upon his own recollections, and the memories of his friends.

'The Norfolk Furies'
Alexander Neville, 1544–1614

Neville was a historian and translator at Cambridge University. He later served under Archbishop Matthew Parker, who deserves notoriety for his hostility to Kett and the rebels. The Norfolk Furies was Neville's major work. It was written under Archbishop Parker's guidance.

'The Chronicles of England, Scotland and Ireland'
Raphael Hollinshed, 1529(?)–1580

An English chronicler, he was one of the contributors to this two-volume work for the printer Reyner Wolfe. It was first published in 1577 after much careful censorship by the Privy Council regarding some parts about Ireland. A second edition was issued in 1587 after 'offensive' pages were removed, again by order of the privy council.

It is reasonable to ask why the chroniclers Sotherton, Neville and Holinshed were so bias in their reporting of the events in the summer of 1549. It surely has to do with their perceptions of their own places in society, and their fear of not being seen to do enough to support the ruling class. John Dudley's delay in Norwich for some time after the end of the rebellion was long enough for him to ensure that records of his actions would be favourable to him and beyond fault in the eyes of his fellow members of the Privy Council, for their assemblies were a hot bed of intrigue and back stabbing. Any report would be scrutinised by them, as they looked for reasons to criticise his campaign. John Dudley had to watch his own back, but so too did any scribe recording the words and actions of the ruling class. The influence Dudley had over Sotherton's writing could only have been when Sotherton was making an early draft of it, while Dudley was still in the city. Dudley remained in the city for about fourteen days, but had left by 8th September. It is thought that Sotherton published his work within ten years following the rebellion. Drafts prepared later by Neville and Hollinshed were guided by the Privy Council and Archbishop Parker. If only the chroniclers had felt safe enough to write the truth, or had not themselves been so class conscious, bias and vitriolic about the rebels and their cause, or if Robert Kett had been able to leave us his version of the story.

The purpose of this book is to spotlight those parts of Sotherton's and other chronicles that clearly avoided or masked the truth about the rebellion. Sotherton's tendency to emphasise the achievements and skill of Warwick's men and officers, while degrading all that was done by the rebels, justifies us in assuming there was much exaggeration throughout his chronicle. Summarised on the following page are my challenges and explanations.

THE DECEPTIONS

1. 'With the Herald... there departed into the city a great number that received the pardon...'

With the deceit and obvious exaggerations by Sotherton in mind, we may rightly assume that the number of rebels who accepted offers of pardon from the King's Herald York and deserted to Royal authority then and at other times were probably far fewer than Sotherton and other chronicles stated.

2. Neville; (the rebels) 'vile rabble'... 'the 'scum of the earth...'

The North Elmham contingent were not all from a poor social level, as indicated by such figures as the Parish Constable. The two representatives in Kett's Government from each of the 'Hundreds' were certainly of similarly 'good social standing' as were a high proportion of the rebels they each represented. Disillusioned soldiers and navy personnel who joined the rebellion were well trained and well disciplined; tough, but not 'scum' or 'vile rabble'.

3. Sotherton; 'A very large and goodly place...' Neville; (rebels) '...marks of their villainies in that once stately house.'

However, Mount Surrey had been deserted for some years, and was probably quite dilapidated at that time.

4. 'Warwick's forces blockaded the rebel camp...'

This was unlikely. It is much more plausible that the rebels blockaded the city, but Warwick could not allow that to be believed so he ordered that the blockading story be turned on its head. Blockading a walled city is relatively easy to do when most of its gates are locked and earth-ramped, leaving only a few that could be opened for supplies; whereas the boundary of the rebel camp was extensive with a multitude of access and supply points.

5. Some rebels deserted to tend their land and livestock...

Few had livestock to tend. Their field strips and grazing land on the 'commons' had been enclosed, and there was little to harvest on the farms, therefore few 'ploughs to follow.'

6. The rebels had little more than pitchforks as weapons...

Only at the beginning of their campaign. All that changed as the rebel army and the range and quantity of their weapons grew.

7. The rebel capture of Warwick's ordnance...

This was not an opportunist or chance action. Spies reported the ordnance entering St. Benedict's, and the rebel leaders reasoned that on that route there was only one viable location intended for the guns; the Benedictine ruins, which offered a clear line of sight to their rebel camp. The rebels ambushed the train in Tombland. The wagon drivers may not have lost their way entirely. That was most probably a cover story to hide the fact that an important action was thwarted by the rebels.

8. Some forward thinking by the rebel leaders...

By their August 25th incursion through the North Wall at Bull Close, the rebels tested the route and the viability of yet another invasion should they be successful in the final battle. The incursion was not simply an incidental action.

9. Out of kindness, Warwick kept his English troops in the city, so that they should not face 'their own kind' in combat...

In truth, he needed to keep a backup reserve close at hand in the city, as a fall-back force to resist another invasion by the rebels.

10. The battle was quickly won...

Not according to Ambrose Dudley, who was on the battlefield.

Walk where the rebels marched to battle

The first half of the walk is on level ground, the rest is gently down hill. An easy stroll for you in daylight, but think of the rebels laden with heavy weapons, leading teams of horses hauling carts and cannons, finding their way in the poor light of early dawn, and in places through dense woodland. You will walk on smooth paving and tarmac; they marched along rough tracks.

Begin in Quebec Road (1). Nearby are raised earthworks (2), the only visible remaining evidence of the rebels' enormous camp. Walk east along Wolfe Road (3) to its junction with Montcalm Road (4), the rebel marshalling area. Look south along Montcalm Road and see the water tower, said to be near the site of the Reformation Oak. Then turn to the north and walk along the shorter stretch of Britannia Road (5) to its junction with Plumstead Road (6). Cross carefully into the longer stretch of Britannia Road (7) and continue to Gurney Road (8). *Warning;* here the rebels were able to march straight across (marked as a thin dashed line) and through what is now the Lavengro housing estate (L), but you should walk a little to the right (9) to where it is safer to cross Gurney Road (8).

But even here, take care at this pedestrian blind spot.

Turn left onto Mousehold Avenue (10) and pass Mousehold First School (11). Near the turn into Gertrude Road (12) you will see the grassy knoll I have named Kett's Point (13) where Kett and his fellow leaders had a clear view over the city. (At the time of writing, trees and bushes crowned the top and obscured the view.) From there continue along the left hand footpath a little further down Mousehold Avenue and look to your right into Crome Road (14). Here was Kett's Gun platform. Continue down and cross Silver Road (15) into Beaconsfield Road (16). In this area, then a plain hillside, the rebels prepared for battle. Continue down to Magdalen Road (17) where they set their lines of 'Shield Wall' stakes from Bull Close (18) to Sprowston Road (19). (Shown in a bold dotted line, S.) Now imagine a few half timbered houses to your left near Magdalen Gate (20) but nothing opposite, just open ground westward, all the way to 'Catton Vale' where Warwick's forces lined up for battle.

Enjoy your walk, but spare a thought for Kett and his doomed rebels.

ACKNOWLEDGEMENTS

My grateful thanks to these helpful people:

- Christopher Sansom, author of the 'Shardlake' historical novels, for his enlightening ideas and helpful comments.
- Adrian and Anne Hoare, helpful friends and fellow Kett enthusiasts.
- Peter Kent of Cupola Books in Norwich for his many helpful suggestions.
- Henry Layte of the 'The Book Hive' in Norwich for his suggestions regarding publication.
- Andy Bennett, interpreter at Norwich Castle Museum, for his advice about Tudor weapons.
- Philip A. Magrath, Curator of Artillery at the Royal Armouries Museum Fort Nelson.
- Personnel of Her Majesties Armed Forces and the Ministry of Defence, for their guidance about military strategies.

REFERENCES

The Commoyson in Norfolk 1549. Nicholas Sotherton (14??–1540?) Edited by Susan Yaxley of Larks Press
The Norfolk Furies. Alexander Neville (1544–1614)
The Chronicles of England, Scotland and Ireland. Raphael Hollinshed (1529?–1580), a contributor.
The History of the City of Norwich Francis Blomefield. Published in 1806
Views of the Gates of Norwich. Robert Fitch FSA, FGS etc., Cundal. Published 1861
If Stones Could Speak. R. H. Mottram, Museum Press. Published 1955
An Historical Atlas of Norfolk. Norfolk Museums Service. Published in 1994
Bryant's Map of Norfolk in 1826. Introduction by J. C. Barringer. Larks Press Edition, 1998
Faden's Map of Norfolk. Introduction by J. C. Barringer, M.A. Larks Press Edition, 1989

RECOMMENDED FURTHER READING

The 1549 rebellions and the making of early modern England. Andy Wood, Cambridge University Press. Published 2007.
On the trail of Kett's Rebellion in Norfolk 1549 Adrian Hoare Published 2016
An unlikely rebel. Robert Kett and the Norfolk Rising, 1549. Adrian Hoare. Published 1999
Robert Kett and the Norfolk Rising. Joseph Clayton. New edition edited by Claire Dollman. Published 2010
Robert Kett. Guy N. Pocock. Published 1926

'I did well in Mr. Kett's camp;
he trusted to see a new day
for such as I.'

Ralph Claxton, a rebel.

'...THIS MEMORIAL WAS PLACED HERE BY THE CITIZENS OF NORWICH IN REPARATION AND HONOUR TO A NOTABLE AND COURAGEOUS LEADER IN THE LONG STRUGGLE OF THE COMMON PEOPLE OF ENGLAND TO ESCAPE FROM A SERVILE LIFE INTO THE FREEDOM OF JUST CONDITIONS.'

At the entrance to Norwich Castle

What would Robert Kett think if he were among us now?
In sorrow he would learn that for many good people of our time,
that long struggle goes on.